The
Senses
of
Walden

An Expanded
Edition

Stanley Cavell

North Point Press
San Francisco
1981

THE SENSES OF WALDEN was first published in 1972 by
The Viking Press and is reprinted with their permis-
sion. "Thinking of Emerson" was first published in
New Literary History in 1979 by The University of
Virginia. "An Emerson Mood" was delivered as the
Scholar's Day Address at Kalamazoo College in 1980.

To
Michael Fried,
John Harbison
and
Seymour Shifrin

Acknowledgments

The initial versions of these chapters were given as Gauss Seminars at Princeton University in February 1971. Later versions were read at Wesleyan University in April of the same year and at the University of California at Santa Barbara in January 1972. Chapter I was the basis of the Raphael Demos Memorial Lecture delivered at Vanderbilt University in November 1971.

All readers of Thoreau owe thanks to Walter Harding's notes in his edition called *The Variorum Walden* and to James Lyndon Shanley's sorting of the *Walden* manuscript, recorded in his *The Making of Walden*. Of the secondary material I have read on Thoreau, I know that I have explicitly responded to the pages devoted to him in R. W. B. Lewis' *The American Adam* and in Richard Poirier's *A World Elsewhere*. In my remarks

vii

about Romanticism I have been helped explicitly by M. H. Abrams' *The Mirror and the Lamp* and his paper "English Romanticism: The Spirit of the Age," which occurs in *Romanticism Reconsidered*, edited by Northrop Frye; and by Geoffrey Hartman's *Wordsworth's Poetry, 1787–1814*. Most generally, I have put myself as deeply in debt as my present resources permit to Perry Miller's *From Colony to Province* as well as to other of his writings about the development of American consciousness, and to Northrop Frye's *Anatomy of Criticism* and to his study of Blake, *Fearful Symmetry*. The sentence on page one is from Thoreau's *Correspondence*. I ought to cite Charles R. Anderson's *The Magic Circle of Walden* as my source for Emerson's remark, to his journal, about the nervousness and wretchedness reading Thoreau could cause him. I should also like to register my awareness that my emphasis on the topic of *Walden*'s reader was encouraged by the attention paid to the topic of the reader in the writings and conversations of Wolfgang Iser and of Lowry Nelson.

I have been fortunate in the audiences that have attended my various readings of earlier stages of these chapters. The manuscript underwent specific changes as a result of discussions at Princeton with Amelie Rorty and Richard Rorty, and at Wesleyan with Victor Gourevitch and Louis Mink. It is a pleasure to remember and to record the seriousness and instructiveness of the students with whom I broached the study of *Walden* — at the Indiana University School of Letters in the summer of 1969, and in a humanities course at Harvard in the spring of 1970.

I am grateful to the director of the Gauss Seminars, Professor Joseph Frank, for his invitation to try out this material in so congenial a context.

This book was written during my tenure as a Fellow of Wesleyan University's Center for the Humanities in 1970–1971. That year of freedom to write, together with the encouragement and example of the community of scholars in and around the Center, have put me permanently yet happily in its debt.

S. C.

Emerson Hall
Cambridge, Massachusetts
May 6, 1972

Contents

Preface

What hope is there in a book about a book? My interest in this question of criticism, as I wrote my book about *Walden*, lay in determining why *Walden* is itself about a book, about its own writing and reading; and in entering certain experiments to determine how one philosophical text is prompted by another, why the history of philosophy is a history of such promptings, and what, accordingly, constitutes an original, or initiating, text. From this perspective, *Walden* appeared and appealed to me in a succession of lights. It was written in an, as it were, pre-philosophical moment of its culture, a moment as yet primitive with respect to the sophistication or professionalization of philosophy, when philosophy and literature and theology (and politics and economics) had not isolated themselves out from one another but when these divorcements could be felt as imminent, for better or worse. This pre-philosophical moment, measured in American time, occurred before the German and the English traditions of philosophy began to shun one another, and I hoped that if I could show *Walden* to cross my own philosophical site, I might thereby re-enact an old exchange between these traditions. (I assume the rhyming of some of the concepts I emphasize — e.g., those of the stranger, of the teacher, of the everyday, of dawning and clearing and resolution — with concepts at play in Nietzsche and in Heidegger.)

I have been asked, concerning my treatment of the dissociation of writing from speaking, what relation I propose between things I have said and things implied in the idea of literature as *écriture*, as this is broached in the writings of Jacques Derrida and Lévi-Strauss. For a while I thought I should say something about this in this book, but I finally thought the attempt would be misguided there, for several reasons: (1) What I had to say about *Walden*'s declaration of writing as such was formed before my acquaintance with the pertinent views of these authors, so it seemed to me that it would be irrelevant or presumptuous to engage in a philosophical dispute over an issue that *Walden* would merely illustrate and not inspire. (2) I do not yet know or understand the pertinent views of these authors well enough to dispute or agree with them. If, for example, they imply that the written word (as opposed to the spoken) is retrograde as the vehicle of cultural expression (as opposed to cultured), then I do not agree, and certainly the writer of *Walden* does not agree. Both currents of expression had become, to his mind, equally retrograde and forward-looking. His insistence on writing as such was not meant to mystify his thought and so protect it from the vulgar; it was meant, on the contrary, to demonstrate the fearful esotericism of his culture's parlance as it stood, to preserve its words against its demented wish to damage and deny them — as if his audience were not illiterate but dysphasic. (3) My remarks about writing as such are not meant as generalities concerning all of literature but as specific acknowledgments of the intention of this writer in this book, in particular two phases of this intention: to rest his achievement of the condition of writing as such specifically upon his achievement of a genuine Scripture; and to alarm his culture by refusing it his voice, i.e., by withholding his consent both from society so called and from what I call "conspiracies" of despairing silence which prevent that society from being his, or anyone's. This refusal is not in fact, though it is in depiction, a withdrawal; it is a confrontation, a return, a constant turning upon his neighbors. This means, first, that he has had to establish himself as a neighbor; which next means, to establish himself as a stranger; which in turn means to establish the concept and the recognition of neighbors and strangers; this will mean establishing his reader as his stranger.

Note (1980)

The two essays on Emerson that the North Point edition enables me to add to *The Senses of Walden* express my continuing indebtedness to the writing of that book better than any new words of introduction are likely to do. The occasion of the first essay, "Thinking of Emerson," is explained in its introductory note. The occasion of the second, "An Emerson Mood," was an invitation to deliver the Scholar's Day Address at Kalamazoo College, January 25, 1980.

For all our life should be baptism, and the fulfilling of the sign, or sacrament, of baptism; we have been set free from all else and wholly given over to baptism alone, that is, to death and resurrection. This glorious liberty of ours, and this understanding of baptism have been carried captive in our day.

MARTIN LUTHER

The Senses of Walden

On the first perusal
plain common sense should appear
— on the second severe truth
— and on a third
severe beauty.

Words

The very greatest masterpieces, when one is fresh from them, are apt to seem neglected. At such a time one knows, without stint, how unspeakably better they are than anything that can be said about them. An essential portion of the teaching of *Walden* is a full account of its all but inevitable neglect.

I assume that however else one understands Thoreau's topics and projects it is as a writer that he is finally to be known. But the easier that has become to accept, the more difficult it becomes to understand why his words about writing in *Walden* are not (so far as I know) systematically used in making out what kind of book he had undertaken to write, and achieved. It may be that the presence of his mysterious journals has too often attracted his serious critics to canvass there for the interpretation of *Walden*'s mysteries. My opening hypothesis is that this book is perfectly complete, that it means in every word it says, and that it is fully sensible of its mysteries and fully open about them.

Let us begin to read in an obvious place, taking our first bearings, and setting some standards, by looking at his explicit directions in the early chapter entitled "Reading." "The heroic books, even if printed in the character of our mother tongue, will always be in a language dead to degenerate times; and we must laboriously seek the meaning of each word and line, conjecturing a larger sense than common use permits out of what wisdom and valor and generosity we have" (III, 3).* This may sound like a pious sentiment, one of those sentences that old-fashioned critics or book clubs like to cite to express their high-mindedness. But it is the first step in entertaining Thoreau's intentions and ambitions to understand that he is there describing the pages he has himself readied for our hands. This may not be obvious at first, because the very extremity of his praise for what he calls "classics" and for "reading, in a high sense," together with his devotion to the "ancients," seems to imply that the making of such a book, a heroic book, in the America he depicts and in "this restless, nervous, bustling, trivial nineteenth century" (XVIII, 14), is not a feasible enterprise. But it is axiomatic in *Walden* that its author praises nothing that he has not experienced and calls nothing impossible that he has not tried. More specifically, what is read in a high sense is "what we have to stand on tiptoe to read and

* To make my references to *Walden* independent of any particular edition, I shall give citations by chapter and paragraph, roman numerals for the former, arabic for the latter. References to "Civil Disobedience" are also according to paragraph, preceded by "CD."

devote our most alert and wakeful hours to" (III, 7); and again, "There are probably words addressed to our condition exactly, which, if we could really hear and understand, would be more salutary than the morning or the spring to our lives" (III, 11). Given the appearance of morning and spring in this book, what words could be *more* salutary than these? But then, given such words in the book as, "Morning is when I am awake and there is dawn in me" (II, 14), we recognize that morning may not be caused by sunrise, and may not happen at all. To discover how to earn and spend our most wakeful hours — whatever we are doing — is the task of *Walden* as a whole; it follows that its task, for us who are reading, is epitomized in discovering what reading in a high sense is and, in particular, if *Walden* is a heroic book, what reading *Walden* is. For the writer of *Walden*, its task is epitomized in discovering what writing is and, in particular, what writing *Walden* is.

It is hard to keep in mind that the hero of this book is its writer. I do not mean that it is about Henry David Thoreau, a writer, who lies buried in Concord, Massachusetts — though that is true enough. I mean that the "I" of the book declares himself to be a writer. This is hard to keep in mind because we seem to be shown this hero doing everything under the sun but, except very infrequently, writing. It takes a while to recognize that each of his actions is the act of a writer, that every word in which he identifies himself or describes his work and his world is the identification and description of what he understands his literary enterprise to require. If this seems to reduce the stature of what he calls his experiment, that is perhaps because we have a reduced view of what such an enterprise may be.

The obvious meaning of the phrase "heroic book," supported by the mention of Homer and Virgil (III, 6), is "a book about a hero," an epic. The writer is aligning himself with the major tradition of English poetry, whose most ambitious progeny, at least since Milton, had been haunted by the call for a modern epic, for a heroic book which was at once a renewed instruction of the nation in its ideals, and a standing proof of its resources of poetry. For the first generation of Romantics, the parent generation to Thoreau's, the immediate epic event whose power their literary epic would have to absorb, was the French Revolution — the whole hope of it in their adolescence, and the scattered hopes in their maturity. The writer of *Walden* alludes to the three revolutions most resonant for his time. Of the Puritan revolution he says that it was "almost the last significant scrap of news" from England (II, 19). Why almost? We don't really need a key for this, but Thoreau provides one in an essay on Carlyle which he wrote while living at Walden: "What . . . has been English news for so long a season? What . . . of late years, has been England to us — to us who read books, we mean? Unless we remembered it as the scene where the age of Wordsworth was spending itself, and a few younger muses were trying their wings. . . . Carlyle alone, since the death of Coleridge, has kept the promise of England." As against the usual views about Thoreau's hatred of society and his fancied private declaration of independence from it, it is worth hearing him from the outset publicly accept a nation's promise, identify the significant news of a nation with the state of its promise, and place the keeping of that promise in the hands of a few writers.

Of the events which keep burning on the Continent, the writer of *Walden* is apparently dismissive: "If one may judge who rarely looks into the newspapers, nothing new does ever happen in foreign parts, a French revolution not excepted" (II, 19). Marx, at about the same time, puts the point a little differently in his *Eighteenth Brumaire*, suggesting that it is only if you think like a newspaper that you will take the events of 1848 (or 1830) as front-page history; they belong on the theater page, or in the obituaries. But in *Walden*'s way of speaking, its remark also means that *the* French Revolution was not new. For example, the revolution we had here at home happened first, the one that began "two miles south" of where the writer is now sitting, on "our only field known to fame, Concord Battle Ground" (II, 10). For an American poet, placed in that historical locale, the American Revolution is more apt to constitute the absorbing epic event. Only it has two drawbacks: first, it is overshadowed by the epic event of America itself; second, America's revolution never happened. The colonists fought a war against England all right, and they won it. But it was not a war of independence that was won, because we are not free; nor was even secession the outcome, because we have not departed from the conditions England lives under, either in our literature or in our political and economic lives.

I understand the writer of *Walden* to be saying at least these things, in his way, when he announces for the second time the beginning of his "experiment": "When first I took up my abode in the woods, that is, began to spend my nights as well as days there, which, by accident, was on Independence Day, or the Fourth of July,

1845, my house was not finished for winter" (ii, 8).
Good and learned readers, since at least Parrington,
will have such a passage behind them when they describe Thoreau as having written a "transcendental
declaration of independence." But why does the writer
say "by accident"? Merely to mock America's idea of
what independence comes to, and at the same time
ruefully admit that he is, after all, one of us? But he has
been insisting on these things from the beginning.
From *what* is he supposed to have declared his independence? Clearly not from society as such; the book is
riddled with the doings of society. From society's beliefs
and values, then? In a sense — at least independence
from the way society practices those beliefs and values.
But that was what America was for; it is what the
original colonists had in mind.

Earlier, as an introduction to the first time we see the
hero at his experiment, about to describe the building of
his house, he quotes at some length from two accounts,
one contemporary and one nearly contemporary, of the
first shelters the colonists made for themselves to get
them through the first winter in the world which for
them was new (i, 57). We know the specific day in the
specific year on which all the ancestors of New England
took up their abode in the woods. That moment of
origin is the national event reenacted in the events of
Walden, in order this time to do it right, or to prove that
it is impossible; to discover and settle this land, or the
question of this land, once for all. This is one reason
that taking up the abode on the Fourth of July is an
accident.

Any American writer, any American, is apt to respond to that event in one way or another; to the

knowledge that America exists only in its discovery and
its discovery was always an accident; and to the obsession with freedom, and with building new structures
and forming new human beings with new minds to
inhabit them; and to the presentiment that this unpar-
alleled opportunity has been lost forever. The distinction of *Walden*'s writer on this point (shared, I suppose,
by the singer of *Leaves of Grass* and by the survivor in
Moby Dick) lies in the constancy of this mood upon
him, his incarnation, one may call it, of this mood at
once of absolute hope and yet of absolute defeat, his
own and his nation's. His prose must admit this pres-
sure and at every moment resolutely withstand it. It
must live, if it can, pressed between history and heaven:

> In any weather, at any hour of the day or night, I have
> been anxious to improve the nick of time, and notch it
> on my stick too; to stand on the meeting of two eterni-
> ties, the past and the future, which is precisely the
> present moment; to toe that line. (1, 23)

This open acknowledgment of his mysticism, or
rather of the path to it, is also a dedication of his prose
to that path. This is what "and notch it on my stick too"
means — that he is writing it down, that his writing and
his living manifest each other. The editor of *The Variorum Walden*, Walter Harding, is surely right to refer
here to Robinson Crusoe's method of telling time; but
that reference alone does not account for the methods
of *Walden*'s writer, for what he would mean by telling
time, in particular for what he means in claiming to
notch not merely the passing of time but his improvement of it. It is when the writer has just gone over the
succession of farms he had bought in imagination, and

comes to his abode in the woods, that he says, "The present was my next experiment of this kind, which I purpose to describe more at length" (II, 7). Of course he means that the building of his habitation (which is to say, the writing of his book) is his present experiment. He also means what his words say: that the present is his experiment, the discovery of the present, the meeting of two eternities. ("God himself culminates in the present moment" [II, 21].) The most extended moment of the book which puts together the ideas of art and of the presentness which admits eternity, is the closing parable about the artist from Kouroo, the surface of which relates those ideas to the notching of a stick.

To say that the writer reenacts the Great Migration and the inhabitation of this continent by its first settlers is not to suggest that we are to read him for literal alignments between the history of the events in his woods and in theirs. That would miss the significance of both, because the literal events of the Puritan colonization were from the beginning overshadowed by their meaning: it was itself a transcendental act, an attempt to live the idea; you could call it a transcendental declaration of freedom. (In his "Plea for Captain John Brown," Thoreau praised this man once as a Puritan and once as a Transcendentalist.) This means that the writer's claims to privacy, secrecy, and isolation are as problematic, in the achievement and in the depiction of them, as any other of his claims. The more deeply he searches for independence from the Puritans, the more deeply, in every step and every word, he identifies with them — not only in their wild hopes, but in their wild denunciations of their betrayals of those hopes, in what has come to be called their jeremiads. (This is a standing difficulty for America's critics, as for Christianity's; Americans and Christians are prepared to say worse things about their own behavior than an outsider can readily imagine.) His identification extends even to the further meaning of the migration: to perform an experiment, a public demonstration of a truth; to become an example to those from whom they departed; to build, as they said to themselves, "a city on a hill."

This is one way I understand the writer's placing himself "one mile from any neighbor." It was just far enough to be seen clearly. However closely Thoreau's own "literary withdrawal" resembles those of the Romantics, in its need for solitude and for nature, the withdrawal he depicts in *Walden* creates a version of what the Puritan Congregationalists called a member of the church's congregation: a visible saint. On this ground, the audience for the writer's words and acts is the community at large, congregated. His problem, initially and finally, is not to learn what to say to them; that could not be clearer. The problem is to establish his right to declare it.

I have come to trust *Walden* and to trust its accuracy to its intentions when it says: "If you stand right fronting and face to face to a fact, you will see the sun glimmer on both its surfaces, as if it were a cimeter, and feel its sweet edge dividing you through the heart and marrow, and so you will happily conclude your mortal career" (II, 22). I cannot say that this writing always and everywhere brings me to this conclusion. But it often does, often enough so that when it does not I am not quick to determine whether it is failing me, or I it. My subject is nothing apart from sensing the specific weight of these words as they sink; and that means knowing the specific identities of the writer through his metamorphoses, and defining the audiences in me which those identities address, and so create; and hence understanding who I am that I should be called upon in these ways, and who this writer is that he takes his presumption of intimacy and station upon himself. For someone who cannot yield to Thoreau's words, or does not find them to warrant this power to divide him through, my subject will seem empty, even grotesque. Emerson did not quite share this enthusiasm, and yet he knew as well as anyone has known how good a writer Thoreau was, as he proved in his speech at Thoreau's funeral by the sentences he chose to read from the unpublished manuscripts. But in the large of it, the writing made him, as he said to his journal, "nervous and wretched" to read. I find this response also to be accurate and essential to the reading of *Walden*—just not final. (The writer of *Walden* knows how trying his trials can be: "I sometimes try my acquaintances by such tests" [1, 35].)

How far off a final reading is, is something I hope I have already suggested. Every major term I have used or will use in describing *Walden* is a term that is itself in play within the book, part of its subject—e.g., migration, settling, distance, neighborhood, improvement, departure, news, obscurity, clearing, writing, reading, etc. And the next terms we will need in order to explain the first ones will in turn be found subjected to examination in Thoreau's experiment. The book's power of dialectic, of self-comment and self-placement, in the portion and in the whole of it, is as instilled as in Marx or Kierkegaard or Nietzsche, with an equally vertiginous spiraling of idea, irony, wrath, and revulsion.

Once in it, there seems no end; as soon as you have one word to cling to, it fractions or expands into others. This is one reason that he says, "There are more secrets in my trade than in most men's . . . inseparable from its very nature" (1, 23). But we do not yet know much else about that trade.

We started thinking along one line about what the writer of *Walden* calls "heroic books"; and while I take him there to be claiming an epic ambition, the terms in which he might project such an enterprise could not be those of Milton or Blake or Wordsworth. His talent for making a poem could not withstand such terms, and the nation as a whole to which he must speak had yet to acquire it. (He knows from the beginning, for example, that his book will not come in twelve or twenty-four parts.) In Thoreau's adolescence, the call for the creation of an American literature was still at a height: it was to be the final proof of the nation's maturity, proof that its errand among nations had been accomplished, that its specialness had permitted and in turn been proved by an original intelligence. In these circumstances, an epic ambition would be the ambition to compose the nation's *first* epic, so it must represent the bringing of language to the nation, words of its own in which to receive instruction, to assess its faithfulness to its ideal. The call for a new literature came, compounding difficulties, at an inconvenient moment in English literature generally, when it was all a writer like Carlyle could do to keep alive his faith in it. John Stuart Mill, three years younger than Emerson, says in his autobiography that a Romantic poem had helped him recover from the critical depression that preceded his maturity; but once he was recovered, it was Bentham's vision, not

Coleridge's, say, that elicited the devotions of a model intellectual. Matthew Arnold, five years younger than Thoreau, spent a life accommodating to his nation's loss of poetry.

According to the assumption that the chapter on reading is meant as a description of the book before us, the one the writer in it went into the woods to write, it is explicitly said to be a scripture, and the language it is written in is what its writer calls the "father tongue."

> Those who have not learned to read the ancient classics in the language in which they were written must have a very imperfect knowledge of the history of the human race; for it is remarkable that no transcript of them has ever been made into any modern tongue, unless our civilization itself may be regarded as such a transcript. Homer has never yet been printed in English, nor Aeschylus, nor Virgil even, works as refined, as solidly done, and as beautiful almost as the morning itself; for later writers, say what we will of their genius, have rarely, if ever, equaled the elaborate beauty and finish and the lifelong and heroic literary labors of the ancients. . . . That age will be rich indeed when those relics which we call Classics, and the still older and more than classic but even less known Scriptures of the nations, shall have still further accumulated, when the Vaticans shall be filled with Vedas and Zendavestas and Bibles, with Homers and Dantes and Shakespeares, and all the centuries to come shall have successively deposited their trophies in the forum of the world. By such a pile we may hope to scale heaven at last. (III, 6)

The hardest thing to understand or believe about this is that the word "scripture" is fully meant. This writer is writing a sacred text. This commits him, from a religious point of view, to the claim that its words are

revealed, received, and not merely mused. It commits
him, from a literary point of view, to a form that com-
prehends creation, fall, judgment, and redemption;
within it, he will have discretion over how much poetry
to include, and the extent of the moral code he pre-
scribes; and there is room in it for an indefinite amount
of history and for a small epic or two. From a critical
point of view, he must be readable on various, distinct
levels. *Walden* acknowledges this in a characteristic
way: " 'They pretend,' as I hear, 'that the verses of
Kabir have four different senses; illusion, spirit, intellect, and the exoteric doctrine of the Vedas'; but in this
part of the world it is considered a ground for complaint
if a man's writings admit of more than one interpretation" (xviii, 7). (This is characteristic in its orientaliz-
ing of the mundane. There is just one text in the culture
for which he writes that is known to require interpretation on four distinct levels.)

Ways in which these commitments are to be realized
in *Walden* are made specific in the meaning of "father
tongue."

Books must be read as deliberately and reservedly as
they were written. It is not enough even to be able to
speak the language of that nation by which they are
written, for there is a memorable interval between the
spoken and the written language, the language heard
and the language read. The one is commonly transitory,
a sound, a tongue, a dialect merely, almost brutish, and
we learn it unconsciously, like the brutes, of our moth-
ers. The other is the maturity and experience of that; if
that is our mother tongue, this is our father tongue, a
reserved and select expression, too significant to be
heard by the ear, which we must be born again in order
to speak. (iii, 3)

Were it not for certain current fantasies according to which human beings in our time have such things to say to one another that they must invent something beyond the words we know in order to convey them, it would be unnecessary to emphasize that "father tongue" is not a new lexicon or syntax at our disposal, but precisely a rededication to the inescapable and utterly specific syllables upon which we are already disposed. Every word the writer uses will be written so as to acknowledge its own maturity, so as to let it speak for itself; and in a way that holds out its experience to us, allows us to experience it, and allows it to tell us all it knows. "There are probably words addressed to our condition exactly, which, if we could really hear and understand, would be more salutary than the morning. . . ." There are words with our names on them—that is to say, every word in our nomenclature—but their existence is only probable to us, because we are not in a position to bring them home. In loyalty both to the rules of interpreting scripture and to the mother tongue, which is part of our condition, the writer's words must on the first level make literal or historical sense, present the brutest of fact. It is that condition from which, if we are to hear significantly, "we must be born again." A son of man is born of woman; but rebirth, according to our Bible, is the business of the father. So *Walden*'s puns and paradoxes, its fracturing of idiom and twisting of quotation, its drones of fact and flights of impersonation—all are to keep faith at once with the mother and the father, to unite them, and to have the word born in us.

Canonical forms of rebirth are circumcision and baptism. True circumcision is of the heart. It has never been very clear how that is to happen; but of course one ought not to expect otherwise: understanding such circumcision requires that you have undergone it; it is a secret inseparable from its very nature. Perhaps it will happen by a line of words so matured and experienced that you will see the sun glimmer on both its surfaces, as if it were a scimitar, and feel its sweet edge dividing you through the heart. Christ is to come with a sword, and in Revelation the sword is in his mouth, i.e., the sword is words. Of baptism, two moments are called for. The water of Walden Pond is unique, but so is every other body of water, or drop, or place; and as universal. John could have used that water in the wilderness as well as any other. The baptism of water is only a promise of another which is to come, of the spirit, by the word of words. This is immersion not in the water but in the book of Walden.

There is a more direct sense in which scripture is written in the father language: it is the language of the father, the word of God; most particularly it is spoken, or expressed, by prophets.

> Then the word of the Lord came unto me, saying, Before I formed thee in the belly I knew thee; and before thou camest forth out of the womb I sanctified thee, and I ordained thee a prophet unto the nations. Then said I, Ah, Lord God! behold, I cannot speak: for I am a child.
>
> But the Lord said unto me, Say not, I am a child: for thou shalt go to all that I send thee, and whatsoever I command thee, thou shalt speak. . . . Then the Lord put forth his hand, and touched my mouth. And the Lord said unto me, Behold, I have put my words in thy mouth. (Jeremiah 1:4–9)

It is Ezekiel who anticipates most specifically the condition of prophecy in *Walden*:

And he said unto me, Son of man, go, get thee unto the
house of Israel, and speak with my words unto them.
For thou art not sent to a people of a strange speech and
of an hard language, but to the house of Israel; Not to
many people of a strange speech and of an hard language, whose words thou canst not understand. Surely,
had I sent thee to them, they would have hearkened unto
thee. But the house of Israel will not hearken unto thee;
for they will not hearken unto me: for all the house of
Israel are impudent and hardhearted. (Ezekiel 3:4–7)

The world of Ezekiel shares other particular features
with the world of *Walden*: its writer received his inspiration "by waters"; it is written in captivity (what
constitutes our captivity in *Walden* has yet to be out-
lined); it ends with elaborate specifications for the building of a house.

Milton, in *The Reason of Church Government*, trusted
himself to identify with the vocation of Jeremiah and of
the author of Revelation in justifying his right and his
requirement to write as he did, "to claim . . . with good
men and saints" his "right of lamenting"; and he further attested to his sincerity by announcing that in
undertaking this task he was postponing the use of his
particular talent, to compose the nation's epic: " . . . to
fix all the industry and art I could unite to the adorning
of my native tongue; not to make verbal curiosities the
end . . . but to be an interpreter and relater of the best
and sagest things among mine own citizens throughout
this island in the mother dialect. ["For what are the
classics but the noblest recorded thoughts of man?"
(III, 3)]. That what the greatest and choicest wits of
Athens, Rome, or modern Italy, and those Hebrews of
old did for their country, I in my proportion, with this

over and above of being a Christian, might do for mine."

Do we really believe, even when it comes from John Milton, in the seriousness of such an identification and ambition? Or do we believe it, or tolerate it, just because it comes from Milton, who twenty-five years later made good with *Paradise Lost* on some highest promise or other? And if we cannot believe it, is that a skepticism about religion or about literature? And if we may believe it about Milton, would we find it credible that any later writer, and an American to boot, could justly, or sanely, so aspire? Blake's placing of himself on this ground is (though with apparently increasing exceptions) not credited. And by the time Wordsworth finds the seer in the child, the idea of the poet-prophet can conveniently seem to us the sheerest of Romantic conceits.

The writer of *Walden* is not counting on being believed; on the contrary, he converts the problem or condition of belief into a dominant subject of his experiment. As I was suggesting, his very familiarity with the fact that he will not be hearkened to, and his interpretation of it, are immediate identifications with Jeremiah and Ezekiel. His difference from them on this point, religiously speaking, is that the time of prophecy is past; the law has been fulfilled. So for both unbelievers and believers it is a stumbling block that a man should show himself subject to further prophecy. Yet this is New England, whose case rests upon the covenant. It ought to remain accessible to specific identifications with the prophets of the covenant.

The writer of *Walden* establishes his claim upon the prophetic writings of our Scripture by taking upon his

work four of their most general features: (1) their wild
mood-swings between lamentation and hope (because
the position from which they are written is an absolute
knowledge of faithlessness and failure, together with
the absolute knowledge that this is not necessary, not
from God, but self-imposed; and because God's prophets are auditors of the wild mood-swings of God himself); (2) the periodic confusions of their authors'
identities with God's—stuck with the words in their
mouths and not always able to remember how they got
there; (3) their mandate to create wretchedness and
nervousness (because they are "to judge the bloody
city" and "show her all her abominations" [Ezekiel
22:2]); (4) their immense repetitiveness. It cannot, I
think, be denied that *Walden* sometimes seems an enor-
mously long and boring book. (Again, its writer knows
this; again it is part of his subject. "An old-fashioned
man would have lost his senses or died of ennui before
this" [IV, 22]. He is speaking of the lack of domestic
sounds to comfort one in the woods, and he is also
speaking of his book. In particular, he is acknowledging that it is not a novel, with its domestic sounds.) I
understand this response to *Walden* to be a boredom not
of emptiness but of prolonged urgency. Whether you
take this as high praise of a high literary discovery, or as
an excuse of literary lapse, will obviously depend on
how high you place the book's value.

Chapter VII, called "The Bean Field," contains the
writer's most open versions of his scriptural procedures or, as he puts it later, his revisions of mythology
(XIV, 22), because he says there explicitly that he is
growing his beans not to eat but solely in order to get
their message, so to speak: "I was determined to know

beans . . . perchance, as some must work in fields if only
for the sake of tropes and expression, to serve a parable-
maker one day" (VII, 10, 11). He acknowledges that he
is himself the parable-maker whom his work in the field
will serve one day by composing an explicit parable in
which his weeding of the field becomes the actions of
Achilles before Troy:

> A long war, not with cranes, but with weeds, those
> Trojans who had sun and rain and dews on their side.
> Daily the beans saw me come to their rescue armed with
> a hoe, and thin the ranks of their enemies, filling up the
> trenches with weedy dead. Many a lusty crest-waving
> Hector, that towered a whole foot above his crowding
> comrades, fell before my weapon and rolled in the dust.
> (VII, 10)

It is an uncommonly obvious moment; it gives no further significance either to his or to Achilles' behavior. It
has nothing of the force and resonance he can bring to
fable or to the mock-heroic when he wants to — e.g., in
the comparison of his townsmen with Hercules (I, 3),
in the battle of the ants (XII, 12–13), or in the new myth
of the locomotive (IV, 8–10). What the writer is mocking in the obviousness of this parable is parable-making
itself, those moralizings over nature that had become
during the past century a literary pastime, and with
which his writing would be confused. With good reason: whatever else *Walden* is, it certainly depends on
the tradition of topographical poetry — nothing can
outdo its obsession with the seasons of a real place. The
writer acknowledges this, too, in allowing the mock-
ery — it is filially gentle — to point at himself and,
hence, at Transcendentalism generally. This comes out

pointedly in the following paragraph, when, after quoting Sir John Evelyn's "philosophical discourse of earth" and another piece of scientific-pious prose about " 'lay fields which enjoy their sabbath,' " he breaks off abruptly with, "I harvested twelve bushels of beans" (VII, 11).

Less obviously, hoeing serves the writer as a trope — in particular, a metaphor — for writing. In the sentences preceding his little parable of the hoer-hero, the writer has linked these two labors of the hand: "—it will bear some iteration in the account, for there was no little iteration in the labor—" (VII, 10). So the first value of the metaphorical equation of writing and hoeing is that his writing must bear up under repetitiveness. He takes the metaphor further: "making ... invidious distinctions with [my] hoe, leveling whole ranks of one species, and sedulously cultivating another." That is, the writer's power of definition, of dividing, will be death to some, to others birth.

As elsewhere in *Walden*, an explicit fable from a foreign classic signals that another parable is under foot. The over-arching parable of the chapter on "The Bean Field" is one that describes the writer-hoer most literally, one which itself takes harrowing to be (a metaphor of) the effect of words:

> See, I have this day set thee over the nations and over the kingdoms, to root out, and to pull down, and to destroy, and to throw down, to build, and to plant. (Jeremiah 1:10)

Here is the parable-maker he is serving *this* day, whether hoeing or writing. The tropes and expressions for the sake of which he works in his field had already been employed; to perform "for the sake of them" is to perform because of them, in order that it shall be fulfilled as it is written. So of course he can only be serving "perchance." It is only through chance that he has been singled out for this service; the ordination is not his to confer, though it is his to establish. And only perchance will his service have its effect; there is a good chance that it will not.

If it does not work, he will not know why — whether it is his people's immovability, or God's, or his own. He keeps saying he doesn't much like hoeing, or the way he is hoeing; he is as irritated by it as he is by other men's devotion to nothing else but. And in fact the second half of this chapter feels thin and irritable; a bad mood is in it. The writer's assertions of hope or of rebuke do not flex upon themselves and soar, but remain mere assertions, moralizings; it has been a bad harvest for him. He manifests nothing like the equanimity in his later knowledge of harvesting: "The true harvest of my daily life is somewhat as intangible and indescribable as the tints of morning or evening. It is a little star-dust caught, a segment of the rainbow which I have clutched" (XI, 7). In the first part of "The Bean Field" the sun is lighting him to hoe his beans (VII, 4), and it comes back at the end ("We are wont to forget that the sun looks on our cultivated fields and on the prairies and forests without distinction" [VII, 16]). But at the center of the chapter the light of nature had gone bad: " . . . I have sometimes had a vague sense all the day of some sort of itching and disease in the horizon" (VII, 7). This happens "when there was a military turnout of which I was ignorant"; American militarism's conception of patriotism infects even the sky; its present manifestation is the Mexican War. This is not the only time he associates despair with a corrupted idea of patriotism: "I sometimes despair of getting anything quite simple and honest done in this world by the help of men. They would have to be passed through a powerful press first, to squeeze their old notions out of them" (1, 38). But "the great winepress of the wrath of God" (Revelation 14:19) is not perfectly effective. The writer continues: " . . . and there would be someone in the company with a maggot in his head." In *Walden*'s "Conclusion" the "maggot in their heads" is patriotism (XVIII, 2).

The writer's next paragraph is uncharacteristically flat in its irony, totally exempting himself from it. "I felt proud to know that the liberties of Massachusetts and of our fatherland were in such safe keeping; and as I turned to my hoeing again I was filled with an inexpressible confidence, and pursued my labor cheerfully with a calm trust in the future" (VII, 8). His mood of mock vainglory persists, and it produces perhaps the most revolting image in the book: "But sometimes it was a really noble and inspiring strain that reached these woods, and the trumpet that sings of fame, and I felt as if I could spit a Mexican with a good relish" (VII, 9). That is, our bayonets in Mexico are the utensils of cannibals.

He acknowledges this despairing, revolted mood a page or so later when he again picks up the tilling theme from Jeremiah, this time with a didactically explicit acceptance of that identity:

> I said to myself, I will not plant beans and corn with so much industry another summer, but such seeds, if the seed is not lost, as sincerity, truth, simplicity, faith, innocence, and the like, and see if they will not grow in

this soil, even with less toil and manurance, and sustain me, for surely it has not been exhausted for these crops. Alas! I said this to myself; but now another summer is gone, and another, and another, and I am obliged to say to you, Reader, that the seeds which I planted, if indeed they *were* seeds of those virtues, were wormeaten or had lost their vitality, and so did not come up. (VII, 15)

It is when Jeremiah is momentarily free of God's voice, and hence of the ordainment to speak to kingdoms and nations, that he says, and hence says to himself:

> When I would comfort myself against sorrow, my heart is faint in me. Behold the voice of the cry of the daughter of my people because of them that dwell in a far country: Is not the Lord in Zion? is not her king in her? Why have they provoked me to anger with their graven images, and with strange vanities? The harvest is past, the summer is ended, and we are not saved. (Jeremiah 8:18–20)

"Alas! I said this to myself": What he said to himself was, Alas!—and alas, that I can say it only to myself. The writer knows that "he that ploweth should plow in hope" (1 Corinthians 9:10). But he has also known, from the beginning, that he is unable to follow that injunction faithfully: " . . . the same sun which ripens my beans illumines at once a system of earths like ours. If I had remembered this it would have prevented some mistakes. This was not the light in which I hoed them" (1, 13).

Hoeing is identified not just with the content and effect of words; it is also an emblem of the physical act of writing, as though the sheer fact that a thing is written is as important as what is said. For the writer's hoe, the earth is a page; with it, the tiller "[makes] the yellow soil express its summer thought in bean leaves and blossoms rather than in wormwood and piper and millet grass, making the earth say beans instead of grass" (VII, 4). This is figured when the artist from Kouroo writes a name in the sand with the point of his stick. The underlying idea of nature as a book is familiar enough; in Bacon, it justifies the scientific study of nature; in Deism, it might be used to ornament a teleological argument for the existence of God. But for an Ezekiel, let us say, these are hardly the issues. In what we call spring, and what the writer of *Walden* shows to be an Apocalypse, bringing his life in the woods to an end, the vision of blood and excrement is transformed into a vision of the earth and its dependents in a crisis of foliation; these leaves in turn produce a vision of the world as an open book (XVII, 7–9). The idea is literalized when he speaks of "the fine print, the small type, of a meadow mouse" (XIV, 18); or speaks of the snow as reprinting old footsteps "in clear white type alto-relievo" (IX, 9).

But heroic books are themselves a part of nature; "the noblest written words are as commonly as far behind or above the fleeting spoken language as the firmament with its stars is behind the clouds. *There* are the stars, and they who can may read them" (III, 4). It may seem that the writer is placing his idea of the meaning of nature in a different category altogether from the meaning of words when he turns from the chapter called "Reading" to that called "Sounds" and remarks, "Much is published, but little printed" (IV, 1). We know he means that nature is at every instant openly confiding in us, in its largest arrangements and in its smallest sounds, and that it is mostly lost on our writers.

But the remark also describes the ontological condition
of words: the occurrence of a word is the occurrence of
an object whose placement always has a point, and
whose point always lies before and beyond it. "The
volatile truth of our words should continually betray
the inadequacy of the residual statement. Their truth is
instantly *translated*; its literal monument alone remains" (XVIII, 6). ((Wittgenstein in the *Investigations*
(section 432) records a related perception: "Every sign
by itself seems dead."))

This theme is declared as the book opens, in its flat
first sentence: "When I wrote the following pages, or
rather the bulk of them, I lived alone, in the woods, a
mile from any neighbor, in a house which I had built by
myself, on the shore of Walden Pond, in Concord,
Massachusetts, and earned my living by the labor of my
hands only." On a second perusal, this sentence raises
more questions than it answers— about where Concord
is, and what a pond is, and how far a mile is, and who
the neighbor is, and what earning a living is. Now what
is "the bulk" of the pages he wrote? We know that
Thoreau wrote about half of *Walden* during the years in
which his hut was his abode; but *every* page the writer
writes, wherever he is and whatever writing is, is merely, or ontologically, the bulk of writing: the mass or
matter of it, the body or looming of it, its physical
presence. Writing is a labor of the hands. We know
from the third paragraph of the book that labor which is
not the labor of slaves has a finish; and we know, from
what is said about hoeing, that labor at its best "[yields]
an instant and immeasurable crop" (VII, 6). Writing, at
its best, will come to a finish in each mark of meaning,
in each portion and sentence and word. That is why in

reading it "we must laboriously seek the meaning of
every word and line; conjecturing a larger sense...."

We are apt to take this to mean that writing, in a high
sense, writing which is worth heroic reading, is meant
to provide occasions for our conjecturing. That is not
wrong, but it is likely to be lukewarm, a suggestion that
the puns and paradoxes, etc., are tips or goads to us to
read with subtlety and activity, and that we are free to
conjecture the writer's meaning. But in *Walden*, reading is not merely the other side of writing, its eventual
fate; it is another metaphor of writing itself. The writer
cannot invent words as "perpetual suggestions and
provocations"; the written word is already "the choicest
of relics" (III, 3, 5). His calling depends upon his
acceptance of this fact about words, his letting them
come to him from their own region, and then taking
that occasion for inflecting them one way instead of
another then and there, or for refraining from them
then and there; as one may inflect the earth toward
beans instead of grass, or let it alone, as it is before you
are there. The words that the writer raises "out of the
trivialness of the street" (III, 3) are the very words or
phrases or lines used there, by the people there, in
whatever lives they have. This writer's raising of them
to us, by writing them down, is only literally, or etymologically, a matter of style, scratching them in. Raising
them up, to the light, so to speak, is the whole thing he
does, not the adornment of it. The manner is nothing in
comparison with the act. And the labor of raising them
up is itself one of seeking "the meaning of each word
and line," of "conjecturing a larger sense ... out of
what wisdom and valor and generosity" the writer has
(III, 3). Conjecturing is not for the writer, and hence

not for the reader, what we think of as guesswork. It is casting words together and deriving the conclusions of each. This is how his labor of the hands earned his living, whatever it was.

Why is the isolation of the written from the spoken word his understanding of the father tongue? Why is it his realization of the faith of the prophets? That is, how does his understanding of his position — in Concord, Massachusetts, "in the Presidency of Polk, five years before the passage of Webster's Fugitive-Slave Bill" (XII, 14) — take him beyond the knowledge prophets have always had of the ineffectiveness of God's words in their mouths; or take him to a different resolution of his ordainment?

I understand his strategy as an absolute acceptance of Saint Paul's interpretation of Christ's giving "gifts unto men" (Ephesians 4): "I therefore, the prisoner of the Lord, beseech you that ye walk worthy of the vocation wherewith ye are called." According to Paul, the gifts for "the perfecting of the saints, for the work of the ministry, for the edifying of the body of Christ" are divided — among apostles, prophets, evangelists, pastors, and teachers. For the writer of *Walden*, in declaring writing to be such a gift, in such a service, the problem of walking worthy of it is different from, anyway later than, Milton's view of his talent: he must learn not merely what to write, in order that his trust not be buried; he must undertake to write absolutely, to exercise his faith in the very act of marking the word. He puts his hand upon his own mouth.

This fulfillment of his call to prophecy overthrows the mode of the old and the new prophecies of the word — their voicing of it. It directly disobeys the

cardinal motivation of Puritan preaching — that the
word be spoken and confessed aloud. The time for such
prophesying is absolutely over. We have heard it said,
"We shall all stand before the judgment seat of
Christ. . . . every tongue shall confess to God. So then,
every one shall give account of himself to God" (Ro-
mans 14:10–12). But *Walden* shows that we *are* there;
every tongue has confessed what it can; we have heard
everything there is to hear. There were prophets, but
there is no Zion; knowing that, Jesus fulfilled them,
but the kingdom of heaven is not entered into; knowing that, the Founding Fathers brought both testa-
ments to this soil, and there is no America; knowing
that, Jonathan Edwards helped bring forth a Great
Awakening, and we are not awake. The experiment of
man ("We are the subjects of an experiment" [v, 10])
has failed. Not that any of man's dreams may not come
to pass. But there is absolutely no more to be *said* about
them. What is left to us is the accounting. Not a re-
counting, of tales or news; but a document, with each
word a warning and a teaching; a deed, with each word
an act.

This is what those lists of numbers, calibrated to the
half cent, mean in *Walden*. They of course are parodies
of America's methods of evaluation; and they are em-
blems of what the writer wants from writing, as he
keeps insisting in calling his book an *account*. As everywhere else, he undertakes to make the word good. A
true mathematical reckoning of the sort he shows requires that every line be a mark of honesty, that the
lines be complete, omitting no expense or income, and
that there be no mistake in the computation. Spoken
words are calculated to deceive. How are written words
different? The mathematical emblem embodies two

ways. First, it is part of a language which exists *primarily* as notation; its point is not the fixing of a spoken language, which had preceded it, but the fixing of steps, which can thereby be remarked. Second, the notation works only when every mark within it means something, in its look and its sequence. Among written works of art, only of poetry had we expected a commitment to total and transparent meaning, every mark bearing its brunt. The literary ambition of *Walden* is to shoulder the commitment in prose.

This ambition, directed toward the establishing of American literature, had to overcome two standing literary achievements with speech: Wordsworth's attempted redemption of the human voice and of poetry by one another; and America's peculiar exaltation of the oration and the sermon. The task of literature is to rescue the word from both politics and religion. ("God is only the president of the day, and Webster is his orator" (XVIII, 14). Even Emerson, in his literature of the sermon, has made a false start. However wonderful, it is not a beginning but an end of something. His voice consoles; it is not of warning, and so not of hope.

I will not insist upon it, but I understand the allusion to Emerson in *Walden* to acknowledge this relation to him.

> There was one other with whom I had "solid seasons," long to be remembered, at his house in the village, and who looked in upon me from time to time; but I had no more for society there. (XIV, 23)

It may be the most unremarkable paragraph of the book; not just because it is one of the shortest, but because it contributes nothing to the account of the visitors the writer received. What is it there for? "I had no more for society there," beyond saying that no one else visited him, can be taken as saying that he could give no more time or take no more interest in Emerson's social position, which is all he offered. But this writer knows who Emerson is, his necessity as a presence and as a writer. Why would he take a crack at him? Nor can the paragraph be there merely to make the account complete, for the notching must mark not simply the occurrence of time but the improvement of it. So in this case the act of marking must itself be the improvement. There is an earlier notice of a visitor whose name the writer is "sorry I cannot print... here" (VI, 8). For me, these curiosities come together in Ezekiel's vision which contains the myth of the writer:

> And [God] called to the man clothed with linen, which had the writer's inkhorn by his side; And the Lord said unto him, Go through the midst of the city, through the midst of Jerusalem, and set a mark upon the foreheads of the men that sigh and that cry for all the abominations that be done in the midst thereof.
>
> And to the others he said in mine hearing, Go ye after him through the city, and smite: let not your eye spare, neither have ye pity:... but come not near any man upon whom is the mark.... (Ezekiel 9:3–6)

The writer's nameless marking of Emerson is done in order to preserve him and, simultaneously, to declare that his own writing has the power of life and death in it. America's best writers have offered one another the shock of recognition but not the faith of friendship, not daily belief. Perhaps this is why, or it is because, their voices seem to destroy one another. So they destroy one another for us. How is a tradition to come out of that?

Study of *Walden* would perhaps not have become

such an obsession with me had it not presented itself as a response to questions with which I was already obsessed: Why has America never expressed itself philosophically? Or has it—in the metaphysical riot of its greatest literature? Has the impulse to philosophical speculation been absorbed, or exhausted, by speculation in territory, as in such thoughts as Manifest Destiny? Or are such questions not really intelligible? They are, at any rate, disturbingly like the questions that were asked about American literature before it established itself. In rereading *Walden*, twenty years after first reading it, I seemed to find a book of sufficient intellectual scope and consistency to have established or inspired a tradition of thinking. One reason it did not is that American culture has never really believed in its capacity to produce anything of permanent value— except itself. So it forever overpraises and undervalues its achievements.

How is one to write so as to receive the power of life and death? Shelley's "unacknowledged legislators of the world" still had to be poets; Carlyle saw modern heroes in mere men of letters. For Thoreau these are not answers, but more questions. How is writing to declare its faithfulness to itself, in that power? How is it to rescue language?

My discussion suggests the following direction of answer. Writing—heroic writing, the writing of a nation's scripture—must assume the conditions of language as such; re-experience, as it were, the fact that there is such a thing as language at all and assume responsibility for it—find a way to acknowledge it— until the nation is capable of serious speech again. Writing must assume responsibility, in particular, for

three of the features of the language it lives upon:
(1) that every mark of a language means something in
the language, one thing rather than another; that a
language is totally, systematically meaningful; (2) that
words and their orderings are meant by human beings,
that they contain (or conceal) their beliefs, express (or
deny) their convictions; and (3) that the saying of something when and as it is said is as significant as the
meaning and ordering of the words said.

Until we are capable of serious speech again—i.e.,
are reborn, are men "[speaking] in a waking moment,
to men in their waking moments" (XVIII, 6)—our
words do not carry our conviction, we cannot fully back
them, because either we are careless of our convictions,
or think we haven't any, or imagine they are inexpressible. They are merely unutterable. ("The at present
unutterable things we may find somewhere uttered"
[III, 11]. Perhaps in the words he is now writing.) The
written word, on a page, will have to show that a
particular man set it there, inscribed it, chose, and
made the mark. Set on its page, "carved out of the
breath of life itself" (III, 5), the word must stand for
silence and permanence; that is to say, for conviction.
Until we can speak again, our lives and our language
betray one another; we can grant to neither of them
their full range and autonomy; they mistake their definitions of one another. A written word, as it recurs page
after page, changing its company and modifying its
occasions, must show its integrity under these pres-
sures—as though the fact that all of its occurrences in
the book of pages are simultaneously there, awaiting
one another, demonstrates that our words need not
haunt us. If we learn how to entrust our meaning to a

word, the weight it carries through all its computations will yet prove to be just the weight we will find we wish to give it.

How is a writer to show, or acknowledge, something true of language as such? I have begun in this chapter to answer that question for the writer of *Walden* — according to my reading of him. So another question has arisen: What will it mean to be the reader of such a writer?

Sentences

All the lines of direction I have so far been taking pass through the figure that the reader is given before the opening paragraph of *Walden*, in its epigraph, the only sentence in the book which occurs twice.

> I do not propose to write an ode to dejection, but to brag as lustily as chanticleer in the morning, standing on his roost, if only to wake my neighbors up.

A later description of cockcrowing, in the chapter called "Sounds," is explicit about the grounds of the writer's identification with the cockerel. "He is more indigenous even than the natives," and "Even the sailor on the Atlantic and Pacific is awakened by his voice." If our woods abounded with these birds, "— think of it! It would put nations on the alert"; they are "their lords' clarions." "No wonder that man added this bird to his tame stock" — domesticated it *because* its clear trumpet is too disturbing (IV, 22). ("One would say that even the prophets and redeemers had rather consoled the fears than confirmed the hopes of man" [I, 109].) If they "could be naturalized without being domesticated," "who would not be early to rise, and rise earlier and earlier every successive day of his life, till he became unspeakably healthy, wealthy, and wise?" Ineffably so. This smack at Benjamin Franklin's prophecies for America continues the writer's call for "a little Yankee shrewdness" (I, 44), and acknowledges the American location from which his calls and songs will have to make their way. He has not been sent to a people of a strange speech and of a hard language. Through *Walden*'s Chanticleer, in his bragging, and in his devotion to philosophy and to the tallest tales of the race, its writer takes upon himself the two archetypes of American folklore distinguished by Constance Rourke: the Yankee, and the Gamecock of the Wilderness. From them he takes over the attitude of the trickster and the capacity for sharp exchange and cracking wise; but they, in turn, in entering his world, have their moods and deeds as subjected to its laws of change and of scrutiny as every other character and setting in it.

The traditional bird of philosophy and prophecy is equally present in the chapter on "Sounds." "I rejoice that there are owls" (IV, 20). The writer grants them their old power with "melancholy forebodings" (IV, 18), and handsomely confers his own mark of prophecy upon them — the bespeaking of dawn: " . . . now [i.e., with the coming of night] a more dismal and fitting day dawns" (IV, 20). The owl is not replaced by the rooster, but it is to be followed by it. Late in the book the writer reaffirms the prophetic gift of the owl "in peace [to] await the dawning of his day" (XIV, 17). It is one of his most extended passages of exchanged identities, as he and a barred owl stare at one another through what is at least the better part of an hour, each "endeavoring to realize" the other.

But it is with the crowing gamecock that the identification is as complete as reason will permit. His "shrill sound never roused me from my slumbers" (IV, 22). That is, I was already awake; I am awakened by the same thing that awakens him. The path of this interpretation is worth drawing because it almost pedantically demonstrates a motive for the writer's verbal calculations. The paragraph opens with, "I am not sure that I ever heard the sound of cock-crowing from my clearing"; and the momentum of that sentence invites the understanding of "never roused me" as "I always slept through it." But before that idea is quite formed, you see that it is ridiculous, and then you are thrown back to the opening line again. How can this observer and experimenter and accounter be unsure whether he ever heard the sound of a rooster from his clearing? Perhaps because the sound is so familiar and frequent to his ear, and at once so faint and so unmistakable, that he is not sure it is a sound heard, i.e., that it comes from outside. But then you may find yourself conjecturing whether one is quite sure one hears, or knows, the sound of one's own voice; and at this point one enters into the theme of "unconscious truthfulness" (I, 67), of those "strong and valiant natures, who will mind their own affairs . . . not knowing how they live" (I, 21). Or perhaps the hallucinatory, or mythical, sound—which therefore again is not strictly speaking *heard*—is the *clarity* of Chanticleer; and then one conjectures whether the "clearing," from which he is not sure he heard it, is a place in the woods or is instead an absorbing activity, as of the sky or water, abstracting him from distractions. At this point one enters a new region in which the activites he ascribes to himself are to be understood, e.g., losing, trailing, finding, mining, minding, building, sitting, standing, walking, settling, leaving. The commitment to Chanticleer entitles *Walden* to Chaucer's Nun's Priest's discovery that a tale is epic in which a crower has to learn to keep his mouth shut.

The purity of Chanticleer's prophecy is that he can speak only to waken and to warn; his essential calling is to watch. Only so is the true prophet distinguishable from false prophets (whom Ezekiel calls "foxes"). Anyone who can speak can say the words "Thus saith the Lord," as God is always finding out. But what the false prophet says is " 'Peace, peace,' when there is no peace"; and what he does is to speak "a vision of [his] own heart" (Jeremiah 23:16). It is worth hearing God's logical solution again:

> When I bring the sword upon a land, if the people of the land take a man of their coasts, and set him for their watchman: If when he seeth the sword come upon the land, he blow the trumpet, and warn the people; Then whosoever heareth the sound of the trumpet, and taketh not warning; if the sword come, and take him away, his blood shall be upon his own head. . . . he that taketh warning shall deliver his soul. But if the watchman see the sword come, and blow not the trumpet, and the people be not warned; if the sword come, and take any

person from among them, he is taken away in his iniq-
uity; but his blood will I require at the watchman's
hand. (Ezekiel 33:2–6)

The true prophet must simply go on and on repeating
his note: you have broken the covenant; turn again.
And this warning is not his, but it is from him—his
response upon seeing that "the days are at hand, and
the effect of every vision" (Ezekiel 12:23). It is true that
the major condition of prophecy is not satisfied by the
writer of *Walden*: the people of the land have not taken
this man of their coasts and set him for their watchman.
Indeed, as he says, "Finding that my fellow-citizens
were not likely to offer me any room in the courthouse,
or any curacy or living anywhere else, but I must shift
for myself, I turned my face more exclusively than ever
to the woods, where I was better known" (1, 32). They
did not know who he was. Nevertheless, in listing the
ways he has "desired to spend [his] life" (1, 22), he tells
of days "spent outside the town, trying to hear what
was in the wind, to hear and carry it express!"; and, "At
other times watching from the observatory of some cliff
or tree, to telegraph any new arrival; or waiting at
evening on the hilltops for the sky to fall, that I might
catch something" (1, 26). He cannot speak because the
people of the land have not placed him; but he is
keeping his own part of the bargain.
    Birds generally at Walden seem to have something of
prophecy in them, perhaps because of their instinct for
light, perhaps because of the clarity of their repetitions.
They seem to me to carry moments of the writer's most
intimate identifications, as befits a poet, or a writer in
competition with the nightingale. He declares himself
as such when he calls upon a wingèd cat he had heard

was in the neighborhood; it was not receiving when he went, but "This would have been the right kind of cat for me to keep . . . ; for why should not a poet's cat be winged as well as his horse?" (XII, 15); and again, returning to Walden one year to find the trees further laid waste: "My Muse may be excused if she is silent henceforth. How can you expect the birds to sing when their groves are cut down?" (IX, 24). He is equally explicit about the sparrow: as it has its trill "so had I my chuckle or suppressed warble which he might hear out of my nest" (IV, 2). That is a compliment he pays his prose as a whole, that its responses are natural or instinctive. But it is also a tip that sometimes he is content to rest from his mightier or migratory flights and let his words warble and chuckle to themselves (e.g., pun or alliterate), pleased as it were just with his own notes for company, or, as he puts it elsewhere, humming while he works. In presenting the whippoor-will, he again shows the bird's response to the changes of light, and adds three touches to this self-portrait: its notes "refer" to the setting of the sun that inspires them, and are "about" dawn; four or five of them sometimes sang "by accident one a bar behind another," as though what they were singing was written for them, or dictated; and "Sometimes one would circle round and round me in the woods . . . as if tethered by a string," which reasonably outlines his own progression (IV, 17). In the "Conclusion," he summarizes these alliances: "It is a ridiculous demand which England and America make, that you shall speak so that they can understand you. . . . As if Nature could support but one order of understandings, could not sustain birds as well as quadrupeds, flying as well as creeping things" (XVIII, 6).

The loon is the most inarticulate of these prophets, but dramatically the most impressive. In a long, virtuoso passage about his game with the loon, the writer concludes that the wild laughter, in which the loon "betrayed himself," is "in derision of my efforts, confident of his own resources," and that it was a "calling on the god of loons to aid him" (XII, 17). The loon is glorying in his faith. Saint Paul tried to explain about this to the suspicious Corinthians:

> I say again, Let no man think me a fool; if otherwise, yet as a fool receive me, that I may boast myself a little. That which I speak, I speak it not after the Lord, but as it were foolishly, in this confidence of boasting. Seeing that many glory after the flesh, I will glory also. (II Corinthians 11:16–18)

The writer of Walden suffers this gladly, and uses the loon to exemplify the book's theme of insanity.

For the moment, I concentrate on the other major theme the loon exemplifies when it comes "as usual, to moult and bathe in the pond" (XII, 16). It is hardly necessary to insist on the concept of moulting, and metamorphosis generally, as central to *Walden*; but as elsewhere, it is hard to believe how thoroughly it is meant. Let me recall one or two passages:

> The abdomen under the wings of the butterfly still represents the larva. This is the tidbit which tempts his insectivorous fate. The gross feeder is a man in the larva state; and there are whole nations in that condition, nations without fancy or imagination, whose vast abdomens betray them. (XI, 5)

> I saw a striped snake run into the water, and he lay on the bottom, apparently without inconvenience, as long as I stayed there, or more than a quarter of an hour;

perhaps because he had not yet fairly come out of the
torpid state. It appeared to me that for a like reason men
remain in their present low and primitive condition; but
if they should feel the influence of the spring of springs
arousing them, they would of necessity rise to a higher
and more ethereal life. (I, 60)

By the end of "Solitude," the writer can say, "I am no
more lonely than the loon in the pond that laughs so
loud" (V, 15) — thus directly answering the particular
inquiry about his loneliness which he had reported, at
the beginning, that his townsmen made about his life.

Early in *Walden* the writer indicates how his fables of
nature should be taken by the human creature. Getting
us used to his mythologizing practices, he calls our
garments "our epidermis, or false skin" (I, 37), which
should be changed only as we are changed, not when
the world asks us to change them: "Our moulting
season, like that of the fowls, must be a crisis in our
lives. The loon retires to solitary ponds to spend it" (I,
36). This use of "must be" is a key to his position.
What the imperative means is that our moulting season, unlike that of the fowls, is not a *natural* crisis.
Nature does not manage it for us. So at the heart of this
apparent return to nature, it is not haphazard for him to
say, "Nature is hard to be overcome, but she must be
overcome" (XI, 12). Our nature is to be overcome.
(Society does not have to be overcome, but disobeyed;
but what that means comes later.) At the same time,
nature is the final teacher powerful enough to show us
overcoming. She is, the new Romantic might say, my
antagonist, whose instruction I must win. The times of
the day and the seasons of the year are not referred to by
my instincts; nature is not my habitat, but my exem-
plar, my dream of habitation. In the newest testament,

nature may prompt and bless my redemption; but it does not accomplish it on my behalf. What I have to work out is still my salvation, and still in fear and trembling (cf. Philippians 2:12). The crisis is still mine to spend. The sexualization of nature is as marked as in Milton's Eden.

It is through nature that nature is to be overcome. It is through words that words are to be overcome. (Silence may only be the tying of the tongue, not relinquishing words, but gagging on them. True silence is the untying of the tongue, letting its words go.) To write standing face to face to a fact, as if it were a scimitar whose sweet edge divides you, is to seek not a style of writing but a justness of it, its happy injuries, ecstasies of exactness. The writer's sentences must at each point come to an edge. He has at all times to know simultaneously the detail of what is happening, and what it means to him that it happens only so. A fact has two surfaces because a fact is not merely an event in the world but the assertion of an event, the wording of the world. You can no more tell beforehand whether a line of wording will cleave you than you can tell whether a line of argument will convince you, or an answer raise your laughter. But when it happens, it will feel like a discovery of the *a priori*, a necessity of language, and of the world, coming to light. One had perhaps seen the first stalk of a returning plant asserting itself with patches of snow still holding their ground. Thoreau writes: "So our human life but dies down to its root, and still puts forth its green blade to eternity" (XVII, 13). That these words should lay aside their differences and join upon this ground of sense, proposes a world which mocks the squalor and cowardice of our imaginations. Nature, no more than words, will leave us alone. If we will not be rebuked by them, and instructed, we will be maddened by them, and turn upon them to make them stop.

The writer retired to his solitary pond to spend his moulting season. Neither men nor nature told him *when* to go, when it was upon him, by accident it began on a Fourth of July. Hence he can say, "I left the woods for as good a reason as I went there. Perhaps it seemed to me that I had several more lives to live, and could not spare any more time for that one" (xviii, 4). Of course this is fair warning to those of his readers who will be attracted to his life that they will not find it at his Walden, but must work out their own. And he is gently chiding those of his townsmen who have had their "second birth and peculiar religious experience" (iii, 11) and thereupon imagine that two are enough, or something special. But his "several more lives to live" leaves his plans indefinite. And that is an essential fact about them: "We should live quite laxly and undefined in front. . . . The words which express our faith and piety are not definite" (xviii, 6). What is definite, or what is to be defined, is that he *spent* it there, expended it, the whole of it. That was the point of the experiment; not to learn that life at Walden was marvelous, but to learn to leave it. It will make for more crises. One earns one's life in spending it; only so does one save it. This is the riddle, or you may say the paradox, the book proposes.

We know some reasons why the writer crows *if only* to wake his neighbors up. In a sense, that is his whole motive. But given our senses as they stand, he is likely at best only to succeed in rousing his neighbors to another round of nervous activity. To go further than that, to put nations on the alert, to cause them to be "awakened by their own Genius," to put dawn in them, to give them not merely the fact but the idea of morning and of moulting, especially the knowledge that these are labors and paths of travel, to show them such possibilities in earning a living—for this, he would himself have to become awakened, i.e., the Buddha; and so would they. Short of that, he may still arouse in them a "green . . . interest in their fates" (1, 8). And if he can get attention that far, they may yet at least be warned.

This is the trick of the book's second paragraph:

> I should not obtrude my affairs so much on the notice of my readers if very particular inquiries had not been made by my townsmen concerning my mode of life, which some would call impertinent, though they do not appear to me at all impertinent, but, considering the circumstances, very natural and pertinent. Some have asked what I got to eat; if I did not feel lonesome; if I was not afraid; and the like. Others have been curious to learn what portion of my income I devoted to charitable purposes; and some, who have large families, how many poor children I maintained. I will therefore ask those of my readers who feel no particular interest in me to pardon me if I undertake to answer some of these questions in this book.

We know the first joke: those questions, and ones like them, *are* the book. The underlying joke is the way in which we know that. The writer shows an initial air of fun by modifying the inquiries concerning his life with "which some would call impertinent"—leaving it open whether that refers to the inquiries or the townsmen or the life. His townsmen are not impertinent, because they have no idea what they are asking: they do not know, for example, that in a sense the first paragraph contains a full answer, or enough of an account for someone to find out the rest if he really wants to know; and, in a sense, the answer requires the whole book; and then after that, one will still have to find out for oneself.

His problem — at once philosophical, religious, literary, and, I will argue, political — is to get us to ask the questions, and then to show us that we do not know what we are asking, and then to show us that we have the answer. The fiction is that some unknown people have asked him these prompting questions. Underlying the fiction is the question: Where does the book begin, the bulk of whose pages he wrote in the woods? That is, at what point do we realize that the "I" of the first paragraph, the second word of the book, has merged with the "I" the book is about? Whenever we realize it, what we will realize is that we were from the first *already* reading it, i.e., that is the form the phenomenological appearance of this knowledge will take. The only book we are to be given is this one, and it is now passing in front of us, *being* written as it were.

To get us to ask the questions. That means to fox us into opening our mouths. It is not only Socrates who is characteristically prompted to philosophize when a townsman opens his mouth. And for the same reason as in this book: because, like the loon, and like Chanticleer, and like the fox, we thereby betray ourselves; or, like the writer of this book, we "thus unblushingly publish [our] guilt" (1, 79). Under the circumstances, this is the pertinent first step to knowledge: a good book is one that elicits our conviction, one by whose wisdom we are "convicted" (III, 8).

The writer discovered that to make a book like his, to collect evidence in the experiment, "You only need sit still long enough in some attractive spot in the woods that all its inhabitants may exhibit themselves to you by turns" (XII, 11)—i.e., in succession, and by turning, and perhaps as vaudeville routines, for your pleasure and profit. Whom does he examine at that spot? Who is the neighbor for whom he is crowing? The chapter on "Reading" identifies his readers as students—and himself, consequently, as teacher. Eventually, students will be anyone whose "education is sadly neglected" (III, 12); and one day we might all "become essentially students" (III, 1)—that is, one day we might find out what essential studying is. Before that day, he speaks of his readers in various ways, e.g., as those "who are said to live in New England" (I, 3) and as "the mass of men who are discontented" (I, 21). But who knows where or who these people are? The first fact the writer knows about his readers, and acts on, is that they are reading his pages now: the repetitions of "pages" are capped by his emphasis on those who "have come to this page" (I, 7), who are present at the very word the writer has printed there: then that is where you are living now, and what you are working at, and "[you] know whether [you] are well employed or not" (I, 21).

As the surface of his words challenges us to conjecture and calculate with them, their plain content challenges our right to go on reading them. "Adventure on life now" (I, 20), he tells us. So let's drop the book. But then it is "the adventurous *student*" who is promised something more salutary than the morning or the spring to our lives. So let's stay on the track of this book. But am I well employed *here*? ("A man sits as many risks as he runs" [vi, 17].) And won't that same question recur no matter where I present myself? Does it matter whether I read, say, *Walden*, or go, say, to Walden? And then I realize that I am in no position to answer that question; yet I cannot shake it. The choice to go on reading or not is left absolutely up to me — whether I am to invest interest here or not. Nothing *holds* my interest, no suspense of plot or development of character; the words seem continuously at an end. The writer keeps writing things I know I ought not to have stopped trying to say for myself; and shows me a life there is no reason I do not live. An old-fashioned man would have lost his senses.

The writer keeps my choices in front of me, the ones I am not making and the ones I am. This makes me wretched and nervous. My choices appear as curiosities, and to be getting the better of me. Curiosity grows with every new conjecture we find confirmed in the words. It seems all but an accident that we should discover what they mean. This becomes a mood of our acts of reading altogether: it is an accident, utterly contingent, that we should be present at these words at all. We feel this as the writer's withdrawal from the words on which he had staked his presence; and we feel this as the words' indifference to us, their disinterest in whether we choose to stay with them or not. Every new clarity makes the writer's existence obscurer to us — that is, his willingness to remain obscure. How can he apparently so completely not care, or have made up his mind, that we may not understand? This feeling may begin our almost unbearable sense of his isolation. Did he not feel lonesome? We are asking now. And then we find ourselves, perhaps, alone with a book in our hands, words on a page, at a distance.

Of course, alone is where he wants us. That was his point of origin, and it is to be our point of departure for this experiment, this book of travels, this adventure "to explore the private sea, the Atlantic and Pacific Ocean of one's being alone" (XVIII, 2): he attracts us so that we put ourselves on this spot, and then turns us around, and so loses us. "Not till we are lost, in other words, not till we have lost the world [here he provides a little object lesson in reading] do we begin to find ourselves, and realize where we are and the infinite extent of our relations." And, "not till we are completely lost, or turned around — for a man needs only to be turned around once with his eyes shut in this world to be lost — do we appreciate the vastness and strangeness of Nature" (VIII, 2). The difficulty in keeping us at the point of departure, and on our own, is one reason he says, "I do not suppose that I have attained to obscurity" (XVIII, 8). That is, I do not know whether I have finally been able to leave you sufficiently alone, to make you go far enough to find us both; I cannot assume that I have kept still long enough in my "attractive spot," so I may have frightened some of its inhabitants away. I may have brought them to "feel [some] particular interest in me" (I, 2), without getting them to be interested in themselves. He is facing out the problem of writing altogether. His writing has not attained itself until it has completely absorbed the responsibility for its existence, i.e., for calling upon his neighbors; in the present case, until it is absolutely still, without assertion, without saying anything that requires his reader to take *his* word for what he says. (The words of *Walden* are no more his than the water of Walden.) "I have not attained to obscurity" means that the I, the ego, has not disappeared; and also that he has not reached the secrets of his trade.

Let us go back to those secrets, for he identifies them with his losses, in perhaps his most famously cryptic passage.

> I long ago lost a hound, a bay horse, and a turtledove, and am still on their trail. Many are the travelers I have spoken to concerning them, describing their tracks and what calls they answered to. I have met one or two who had heard the hound, and the tramp of the horse, and even seen the dove disappear behind a cloud, and they seemed as anxious to recover them as if they had lost them themselves. (1, 24)

I have no new proposal to offer about the literary or biographical sources of those symbols. But the very obviousness of the fact that they are symbols, and function within a little myth, seems to me to tell us what we need to know. The writer comes to us from a sense of loss; the myth does not contain more than symbols because it is no set of desired things he has lost, but a connection with things, the track of desire itself. Everything he can list he is putting in his book; it is a record of losses. Not that he has failed to make some gains and have his finds; but they are gone now. He is not present to them now. Or, he is trying to put them behind him, to complete the crisis by writing his way out of it. It is a gain to grow, but humanly it is always a loss of something, a departure. Like any grownup, he has lost childhood; like any American, he has lost a

nation and with it the God of the fathers. He has lost
Walden; call it Paradise; it is everything there is to lose.
The object of faith hides itself from him. Not that he
has given it up, and the hope for it; he is on the track.
He knows where it is to be found, in the true acceptance
of loss, the refusal of any substitute for true recovery.
(The logic, if not quite the message, is the same as
Pascal's: "Shall he who alone knows nature know it
only to his undoing? Shall he who alone knows it live in
solitary misery? He must not see nothing at all; nor
must he see enough to believe that he possesses it; he
must see enough to know that he has lost it; for, to
know his loss, he must see and not see; and that is
precisely his natural condition. Whichever side he
takes I shall not leave him at rest.")

He is not fully recovered. He has come back, "a
sojourner in civilized life again" (I, 1). He was a sojourner there before, and now again he sojourns there
instead of at Walden. This is a likely place to see the
need for *Walden*'s paradoxes. It is natural to take the
words "sojourner in civilized life again" to suggest that
the writer will be returning to Walden, where he was
not sojourning, but at home. That is not false; for one
thing, he is returning in his writing. But in the terms of
his book, the sense in which it is true that he was at
home in Walden is that he learned there how to sojourn,
i.e., spend his day. That life on earth is a test and a
sojourn is hardly news. We merely sometimes forget
what a land of pilgrims means, or forget to discover it.
It is not the writer's invention that to be peregrine is to
be a stranger, any more than it is his fancy that perdi-
tion is the loss of something. He keeps emphasizing
that he is back "in civilized life again" by explicitly

going back within the book to visit Walden — e.g., to measure its height on the shore or to record the day in successive years on which its ice breaks up — as though testing his condition now with conditions there, and with his condition when he abode there.

The little myth of the hound, horse, and turtledove refers to "one or two" — viz., travelers, hence strangers — who had heard and seen what he has lost, and seemed as anxious to recover them as if the losses were theirs. Here the writer fully identifies his audience as those who realize that they have lost the world, i.e., are lost to it. The fate of having a self — of being human — is one in which the self is always to be found, fated to be sought, or not; recognized, or not. My self is something, apparently, toward which I can stand in various relations, ones in which I can stand to other selves, named by the same terms, e.g., love, hate, disgust, acceptance, knowledge, ignorance, faith, pride, shame. In the passage in question, *Walden*'s phenomenological description of finding the self, or the faith of it, is one of trailing and recovery; elsewhere it is voyaging and discovery. This is the writer's interpretation of the injunction to know thyself. His descriptions emphasize that this is a continuous *activity*, not something we may think of as an intellectual preoccupation. It is *placing* ourselves in the world. That you do not know beforehand what you will find is the reason the quest is an experiment or an exploration. The most characteristic of the writer's reflexive descriptions is that of finding himself in some attitude or locale: "I found myself suddenly neighbor to the birds" (ii, 9); "I found myself suddenly in the shadow of a cloud" (x, 3); "I found repeatedly, of late years, that I cannot fish without

falling a little in self-respect" (XI, 5); "I find myself
beginning with the letters *gl*" (IV, 19). The place you
will come to may be black (XVIII, 2), something you
would disown; but if you have found yourself there,
that is so far home; you will either domesticate that,
naturalize yourself there, or you will recover nothing.

It is to those who accept this condition of human
existence that the writer accords the title of traveler or
stranger. It is the first title he accords himself (after
writer). Those to whom he addresses his account are
therefore his "kindred from a distant land" (I, 2). Here
is another underlying perception, or paradox, of *Walden* as a whole — that what is most intimate is what is
furthest away; the realization of "our infinite relations," our kinships, is an endless realization of our
separateness. The simple and sincere account the writer
requires of "every writer, first or last" will come from a
distance because "if he has lived sincerely, it must have
been in a distant land to me." Why take this merely as a
complacent or academic disclaimer of his own sincerity? Of course he will not *claim* to be sincere — what
would be the point? — especially not on the first page of
his voyage; for sincerity is the end, and he only requires
it "first or last." It will turn out that to be sincere,
pure — he will centrally call it chastity — is to find God
(XI, 11); and "How shall a man know if he is chaste? He
shall not know it" (XI, 12). In particular, nothing he
can do, or not do, will prove it. To say that a man who
has lived sincerely "must have been in a distant land to
me" is just an opening definition of sincerity as the
capacity to live in one's own separateness, to sail the
Atlantic and Pacific Ocean of one's being alone.

These thoughts are dramatized in the next paragraph, the book's third: "I would fain say something, not so much concerning the Chinese and Sandwich Islanders as you who read these pages, who are said to live in New England; something about your condition, especially your outward condition or circumstances in this world. . . . I have traveled a good deal in Concord"; and then he goes on to compare his townsmen with Hercules and with Brahmins performing "conscious penance." The surface is clear enough: Concord is stranger to him, and he to it, than the ends of the earth. But why does this watchman of the private sea insist especially on his readers' *outward* condition or circumstances in this world? Because the outward position or circumstance in this world is precisely the position of outwardness, outsideness to the world, distance from it, the position of stranger. The first step in attending to our education is to observe the strangeness of our lives, our estrangement from ourselves, the lack of necessity in what we profess to be necessary. The second step is to grasp the true necessity of human strangeness as such, the opportunity of outwardness.

The writer modulates the theme of outsideness throughout the book. One good summary of his idea occurs in a model of the Ode to Dejection he does not propose to write: ". . . from outward forms to win / The passion and the life, whose fountains are within." Coleridge despairs of victory; Thoreau's proposal is to brag from just that perch of possibility. If only to wake his neighbors up—and not succeed in awakening them to the passion and the life; and not succeed in awakening himself. What he knows is that "The morning wind forever blows, the poem of creation is uninterrupted; but few are the ears that hear it. Olympus is but the

outside of the earth everywhere" (ii, 8). The abode of
the gods is to be entered not merely at the outermost
point of the earth or at the top of the highest mountain,
and maybe not at all; but anywhere, only at the point of
the present.

But just this endless occasion is the constant possibility of dejection, which, in the words of Coleridge, is to
gaze upon beauty, but with a blank eye; to see, and not
to feel it. This is the characteristic threat of prophecy,
and of the knowledge of the gospel: since you have seen
and heard, there is no further sacrifice for you, the
blood will be on your own head. If Thoreau's words
merely show us promises we can never accept, then his
beauty mocks us; he has realized the fear in his epigraph and written an ode to dejection. I take those
words to mean that dejection is the obvious subject to
treat of, the metaphysical condition shared by writer
and reader, here and now, where we live. It is the
condition, as Coleridge shows it, of "grief without a
pang," grief "Which finds no natural outlet, no relief, /
In wood, or sign, or tear—." It is without expression.

This is the vision in *Walden*'s paragraph with the
famous opening line: "The mass of men lead lives of
quiet desperation" (i, 9); the short paragraph harps on
the word "despair," or an inflection of it, six times.
Thoreau proposes not to keep quiet about the despair
any longer. But the bragging, while it will not praise
dejection or melancholy, will recognize how formidable
a foe it is, and hence acknowledge and absorb the Romantic poets' bravery in facing it with their odes. The
bragging and the wild laughter will have to take place
over despair, and perhaps will express only that shrill
sound. Then it may at least wake his neighbors up to
their actual condition.

In the writer's words, as they take on more life, this
condition is explicitly described as a want of expression.

> While such a sun holds out to burn, the vilest sinner may
> return. Through our own recovered innocence we dis-
> cern the innocence of our neighbors. You may have
> known your neighbor yesterday for a thief, a drunkard,
> or a sensualist, and merely pitied or despised him, and
> despaired of the world; but the sun shines bright and
> warm this first spring morning, re-creating the world....
> There is not only an atmosphere of good will about him,
> but even a savor of holiness groping for expression.
> (XVII, 19)

So the secrets of his trade are the ones his neighbors
keep: that they are in despair, which is quiet; and that
there is holiness in them, which gropes, like a blind
man, or a child.

The hymn-form in the first line of this excerpt—not
the book's only activation of the old pun on sun/son—
completes the identification of despair with sin, and
affords the writer his confession of that sin. This ac
knowledgment validates his discernment of his neighbors' condition. "I never dreamed of any enormity
greater than I have committed. I never knew, and never
shall know, a worse man than myself" (1, 107). These
are not presumptuous modesties. They are acceptances
of epistemological fact, necessary limits of knowledge.

The writer will give this double condition (of sin and
innocence, his neighbors' and his own) expression in
the book, if he can. But there are further secrets about
what expression requires:

> Sometimes I heard the foxes as they ranged over the
> snow crust, in moonlight nights, in search of a partridge
> or other game, barking raggedly and demoniacally like

> forest dogs, as if laboring with some anxiety, or seeking
> expression, struggling for light. . . . They seemed to me
> to be rudimental, burrowing men, still standing on their
> defence, awaiting their transformation. Sometimes one
> came near to my window, attracted by my light, barked a
> vulpine curse at me, and then retreated. (xv, 4)

There is a lot in this, a crossroads and summary of
many conceptions. The fox, Chanticleer's adversary, is
related to men by its cursing ("Our hymn books resound with a melodious cursing of God and enduring
him forever" [I, 109]), and related to the man writing
his story by burrowing ("My instinct tells me that my
head is an organ for burrowing" [II, 23]). It is also to
the point that the fox's bark is demonic; that the foxes
are curiously attracted to this writer by his light; and
that it is winter. But for the moment we are looking at
its interpretation of seeking expression, viz., as labor-
ing with anxiety (the travelers were anxious to recover
the bay horse, hound, and turtledove) and, in particular, as awaiting transformation; moulting.

We have noticed that awaiting the word of the father
tongue requires rebirth; and the writer associates the
volatile truth of words, instantly translated from their
graves, with his effort to "lay the foundation of a true
expression" (xviii, 6). Our emphasis here is on the
writer's association of finding expression with a moment of imminent hope and imminent despair. He
enacts this association in a passage that shows him
reading. At the opening of "Brute Neighbors," the
Hermit, accepting an invitation from the Poet to go
fishing, sends him off to dig bait while he comes to the
conclusion of a meditation:

Let me see; where was I? Methinks I was nearly in this frame of mind; the world lay about at this angle. Shall I go to heaven or a-fishing? If I should soon bring this meditation to an end, would another so sweet occasion be likely to offer? I was as near being resolved into the essence of things as ever I was in my life . . . My thoughts have left no track, and I cannot find the path again. . . . I will just try these three sentences of Con-fut-see; they may fetch that state about again. I know not whether it was the dumps or a budding ecstasy. Mem. There never is but one opportunity of a kind. (XII, 5)

This is the condition of serious reading. You need to be prepared to find either state.

A writer in meditation is literally a human being awaiting expression. The writer in *Walden* assumes a larger burden of this waiting than other men may: partly because it is his subject that the word and the reader can only be awakened together; partly because, as once before, there is an unprecedented din of prophecy in the world. Everyone is saying, and anyone can hear, that this is the new world; that we are the new men; that the earth is to be born again; that the past is to be cast off like a skin; that we must learn from children to see again; that every day is the first day of the world; that America is Eden. So how can a word get through whose burden is that we do not understand a word of all this? Or rather, that the way in which we understand it is insane, and we are trying again to buy and bully our way into heaven; that we have failed; that the present is a task and a discovery, not a period of America's privileged history; that we are not free, not whole, and not new, and we know this and are on a downward path of despair because of it; and that for the child to grow he requires family and familiarity, but for a grownup to grow he requires strangeness and transformation, i.e., birth? One of the writer's trades is that of "reporter to a journal, of no very wide circulation" (i, 27). Merely to say that Thoreau refers here to his private journal leaves his devotion to it as mysterious as ever, and fails to compute the pun. The writer is a reporter because what he is writing is news, about the world we have made; in particular, that infinitely more is changing than is realized, and infinitely less.

His immediate problem is not that his account has never been "audited" ("I have not set my heart on that" [i, 30]). His problem is that every line of his account is cause for despair, because each is an expression he has waited for, and yet with each he is not transformed. Within his book, the placement of the epigraph sentence declares that fact:

> The present was my next experiment of this kind, which I purpose to describe more at length, for convenience, putting the experience of two years into one. As I have said, I do not propose to write an ode to dejection but to brag as lustily as chanticleer in the morning, standing on his roost, if only to wake my neighbors up. (ii, 7)

Since "experiment of this kind" directly refers to the possessing of a house, and since that has just before been shown to be, rightly understood, a poetic exercise, the present experiment is the book at hand. "I do not propose to write an ode to dejection" parallels "I purpose to describe more at length": his plan "for convenience, [to] put the experience of two years into one," widely praised as his artistic achievement, is so

far a cause for his despair as a man and as a writer of the
kind he wishes to be. Why is one year better than two?
"The phenomena of the year take place every day in a
pond on a small scale" (xvii, 2). And what is sacred
about a day? The experiment is the present — to make
himself present to each circumstance, at every eventu-
ality; since he is writing, in each significant mark. The
very awareness of time compromises presentness; the
succession of words is itself a rebuke. There never is
but one opportunity of a kind. That is the threat, but
also the promise. To go on, untransformed, unchaste so
far as you know, means that you have not been divided
by the fact and concluded your mortal career. But to
learn to await, in the way you write, and therewith in
every action, is to learn not to despair of opportunity
unforeseen. That was always the knack of faith. Crowing, if it is not followed by the last day, will at any rate
express acceptance of that promise; if there is not dawn
in him, the crower is at any rate studying "an infinite
expectation of the dawn" (ii, 15). He will then simply
glory, if only to reject, to disperse, despair; if only to
remind his neighbors, who themselves are glorying,
that there is a less foolish cause for doing so.

To realize where we are and what we are living for,
the conditions of our present, the angle at which we
stand to the world, the writer calls "improving the
time," using a preacher's phrase and giving his kind of
turn to it. No one's occasions are exactly those of
another, but our conditions of improvement are the
same, especially our outsideness and, hence, the world's
presence to us. And our conditions are to be realized
within each calling, whatever that happens to be. Each
calling — what the writer means (and what anyone

means, more or less) by a "field" of action or labor — is isomorphic with every other. This is why building a house and hoeing and writing and reading (and we could add, walking and preparing food and receiving vistors and giving charity and hammering a nail and surveying the ice) are allegories and measures of one another. All and only true building is edifying. All and only edifying actions are fit for human habitation. Otherwise they do not earn life. If your action, in its field, cannot stand such measurement, it is a sign that the field is not yours. This is the writer's assurance that his writing is not a substitute for his life, but his way of prosecuting it. He writes because he is a writer. This is why we can have the sense, at once, that he is attaching absolute value to his words, and that they do not matter. What matters is that he show in the way he writes his faithfulness to the specific conditions and acts of writing as such.

Faithfulness to writing as such, as it is given to him to write, I have characterized as faithfulness to conditions of language as such. If we now include among these conditions the fact that the writing is to be read, this will establish a different set of occasions for acknowledging those conditions, a different position with respect to them, a different field of action. As the writer must establish or create his mode of presence to the word, he must admit or create the reader's mode of presence to it. It is the ground upon which they will meet.

The reader's position has been specified as that of the stranger. To write to him is to acknowledge that he is outside the words, at a bent arm's length, and alone with the book; that his presence to these words is perfectly contingent, and the choice to stay with them continuously his own; that they are his points of departure and origin. The conditions of meeting upon the word are that we—writer and reader—learn how to depart from them, leave them where they are; and then return to them, find ourselves there again. We have to learn to admit the successiveness of words, their occurrence one after the other; and their permanence in the face of our successions.

The endless computations of the words of *Walden* are part of its rescue of language, its return of it to us, its effort to free us and our language of one another, to discover the autonomy of each. For the word to return, what is necessary is not that we compute complexities around it, and also not exactly that we surround it with simplicities, but that we see the complexities *it* has and the simplicity it may have on a given occasion if we let it. Immediately, this means that we recognize that we have a choice over our words, but not over their meaning. Their meaning is in their language; and our possession of the language is the way we live in it, what we ask of it. ("To imagine a language is to imagine a form of life.") That our meaning a word is our return to it and its return to us—our occurring to one another—is expressed by the word's literality, its being just these letters, just here, rather than any others.

In religion and politics, literality is defeated because we allow our choices to be made for us. In religion our hymn books resound with a cursing of God because the words are used in vain. We are given to say that man's chief end is to glorify God and to enjoy him forever. But we do not let the words assess our lives, we do not mean what they could mean, so what we *do* when we repeat those words becomes the whole meaning of "man," and "chief end," and "glorify," and "God," etc., in our lives; and that is a curse. In politics we allow ourselves to say, e.g., that a man is a fugitive who is merely running from enslavement. That is an attempted choice of meaning, not an autonomous choice of words. Beyond the bondage to institutions, we have put nature in bondage, bound it to our uses and to our hurried capacities for sensing, rather than learning of its autonomy. And this means that an object named does not exist for us in its name. We do not know what the bottom of a pond is if we do not know, e.g., what it is to sound the bottom, vaguely imagining that it is abysmally deep. We do not literally mean that we are searching for "the evening robin, at the end of a New England summer day" where he sings on his twig, unless we mean *him* and *the* twig (XVII, 15). We do not know what "Walden" means unless we know what Walden is. The return of a word requires the recovery of its object for us. This was one quest of Romantic poetry, and of the Kantian project to answer skepticism. In *Walden*, both of the tasks are accepted.

Words come to us from a distance; they were there before we were; we are born into them. Meaning them is accepting that fact of their condition. To discover what is being said to us, as to discover what we are saying, is to discover the precise location from which it is said; to understand why it is said from just there, and at that time. The art of fiction is to teach us distance — that the sources of what is said, the character of whomever says it, is for us to discover. ("Speech is for the convenience of those who are hard of hearing" [VI, 3]. This is not an injunction against speaking, but a definition of speakers, i.e., of mankind.) Speaking together face to face can seem to deny that distance, to deny that facing one another requires acknowledging the presence of the other, revealing our positions, betraying them if need be. But to deny such things is to deny our separateness. And that makes us fictions of one another.

A text which is an account has no audience, or one could say that its audience consists of isolated auditors. To read the text accurately is to assess its computations, to check its sentences against our convictions, to prove the derivation of its words. Since every mark counts, the task is to arrive in turn at each of them, as at conclusions. A deep reading is not one in which you sink away from the surface of the words. Words already engulf us. It is one in which you depart from a given word as from a point of origin; you go deep as into woods. Understanding is a matter of orientation, of bearings, of the ability to keep to a course and to move in natural paths from any point to any other. The depths of the book are nothing apart from its surfaces. Figurations of language can be thought of as ways of reflecting the surfaces and depths of a word onto one another.

I mention two of the writer's characteristic procedures meant to enforce our distance from the words and our presentness to them — to show our hand in accepting or arriving at them. First, there is his insistence on the idea of what we *call* something, or what something is said by us to be. In the opening fifty pages of *Walden* there are a dozen instances of modifications like "so-called" or "what is called." For example: "By a seeming fate, commonly called necessity . . ." (1, 5); "None can be an impartial or wise observer of human life but

from the vantage ground of what *we* should call voluntary poverty" (1, 19); "The cost of a thing is the amount
of what I will call life which is required to be exchanged
for it" (1, 45); "The religion and civilization which are
barbaric and heathenish build splendid temples; but
what you might call Christianity does not" (1, 78). The
meaning of the modification is clear in each context,
and hardly surprising: what is called necessary is commonly a myth; what we call voluntary poverty may in
fact be "simplicity, independence, magnanimity, and
trust"; I will call your labor life, for the sake of argument and so as not to raise too many questions at once;
what you might call Christianity, if you were accurate to
its own criteria, does not exist or is in any case not what
you do call Christianity. The point of modification is to
suggest that our words are our calls or claims upon the
objects and contexts of our world; they show how we
count phenomena, what counts for us. The point is to
get us to withhold a word, to hold ourselves before it, so
that we may assess our allegiance to it, to the criteria in
terms of which we apply it. Our faithlessness to our
language repeats our faithlessness to all our shared
commitments.

A second characteristic procedure by which the
writer of *Walden* enforces the distance and presentness
of words is his construction of sentences whose meaning, in context, requires an emphasis other than, or in
addition to, the one their surface grammar suggests. I
will give some examples of these constructions, without
comment, supplying the emphasis I take the context to
require, and assuming that it will be obvious how each
would otherwise habitually be emphasized: "The *present* was my next experiment of this kind"; "I sometimes

try my acquaintances by such tests"; "It is a ridiculous demand which England and America make, that you shall speak so that *they* can understand you"; "I am a sojourner in *civilized* life again"; "I would fain say something concerning you who are said to *live* in New England"; "I think that we may safely trust a good *deal* more than we do" (1, 15); "the gross but somewhat foreign form of servitude called *Negro* Slavery" (1, 8); "In eternity there is indeed *something* true and sublime" (11, 21); "I do not propose to write an *ode* to dejection"; "I do not *propose* to write an ode to dejection." The fact that different emphases eclipse one another shows our hand in what we choose to say. This mode of controlling ambiguity shows that our mind is chanced, but not forced, by language. The point is to get us to assess our orientation or position toward what we say.

The assessments of our commitment and orientation, the idea of our distance from words and others and of their presence to us, are matters the writer often registers by his extraordinary placements of the word "interest." For example: "It was easy to see that they could not long be companions. . . . They would part at the first interesting crisis in their adventures" (1, 100); "A young man tried for a fortnight to live on hard, raw corn on the ear. . . . The human race is interested in these experiments" (1, 87); "How much more interesting an event is that man's supper who has just been forth in the snow to hunt, nay, you might say, steal, the fuel to cook it with! His bread and meat are sweet" (XIII, 12). It would be a fair summary of the book's motive to say that it invites us to take an interest in our lives, and teaches us how.

If *Walden* is a scripture it must contain a doctrine. (I take its writer to be acknowledging this in saying "I too had woven a kind of basket of a delicate texture" [1, 31]. A set of canonical Buddhist scriptures is called the "Three Baskets.") I have wished to suggest, or predict, a movement from more or less formal questions about the kind of book *Walden* is to matters more or less concerning its doctrine. Before going on to say more consecutively what I can about that, I pause to rehearse what I think of as the book's low myth of the reader. It may be thought of as a one-sentence fabliau: The writer has been describing the early spring days in which he went down to the woods to cut down timber for his intended house; he depicts himself carrying along his dinner of bread and butter wrapped in a newspaper which, while he was resting, he read. A little later he says:

> In those days, when my hands were much employed, I read but little, but the least scraps of paper which lay on the ground, my holder, or tablecloth, afforded me as much entertainment, in fact answered the same purpose as the Iliad. (1, 65)

If you do not know what reading can be, you might as well use the pages of the *Iliad* for the purpose for which newspaper is used after a meal in the woods. If, however, you are prepared to read, then a fragment of newspaper, discovered words, are sufficient promptings, bespeaking distant and kindred lives and deaths. The events in a newspaper, our current lives, are epic, and point morals, if we know how to interpret them. The words of the *Iliad* should come to us as immediately as election results or rumors of war.

I kept Homer's Iliad on my table through the summer,
though I looked at his page only now and then. Incessant
labor with my hands, at first, for I had my house to finish
and my beans to hoe at the same time, made more study
impossible. (III, 2)

More study than what? More than looking at Homer's
page now and then or more than hoeing his beans? ("I
did not read books the first summer; I hoed beans" [IV,
2].) From his description, I picture the book lying open
on the table. Could looking at a page now and then,
under any circumstances, constitute study? If not, how
would turning the pages help?

Portions

I have spoken of the sense of loss and of the vision of general despair which *Walden* depicts in its early pages, and of the crowing and trickery of the book as taking place over them or in the face of them. Despair and a sense of loss are not static conditions, but goads to our continuous labor: "That man who does not believe that each day contains an earlier, more sacred and auroral hour than he has yet profaned, has despaired of life, and is pursuing a descending and darkening way" (ii, 14). It is not merely the company of others that causes this. Going to Walden, for example, will not necessarily help you out, for there is no reason to think you will go there and live there any differently from the way you are going on now. "From the desperate city you go into the desperate country, and have to console yourself with the bravery of minks and muskrats" (i, 9). "How to migrate thither" is the question. We are living "what is not life" (II, 16), *pursuing* a descending and darkening way. And yet to realize his wish to live deliberately the writer went "*down* to the woods" (VIII, 3). And downward is the direction he invites us in:

> Let us settle ourselves, and work and wedge our feet downward through the mud and slush of opinion, and prejudice, and tradition, and delusion, and appearance, that alluvion which covers the globe, through Paris and London, through New York and Boston and Concord, through church and state, through poetry and philosophy and religion, till we come to a hard bottom and rocks in place, which we can call *reality*, and say, This is, and no mistake; and then begin, having a *point d'appui*, below freshet and frost and fire, a place where you might found a wall or a state. . . . Be it life or death, we crave only reality. (II, 22)

The path to a point of support and origin is not immediately attractive, but the hope in it, and the hope that we can take it, is exactly that we are *living* another way, pursuing death, desperate wherever we are; so that if we could go all the way, go *through* Paris and London, *through* church and state, *through* poetry and philosophy and religion, we might despair of despair itself, rather than of life, and cast *that* off, and begin, and so reverse our direction.

He introduces his invitation to voyage as a matter of "settling ourselves." At the end:

> I love to weigh, to settle, to gravitate toward that which most strongly and rightfully attracts me . . . not suppose a case, but take the case that is; to travel the only path I can, and that on which no power can resist me. It affords

me no satisfaction to commence to spring an arch before
I have got a solid foundation. . . . There is a solid bottom
everywhere. (XVIII, 14)

Settling has to do with weighing, then; and so does
deliberating, pondering. To live deliberately would be
to settle, to let ourselves clarify, and find our footing.
And weighing is not just carrying weight, by your force
of character and in your words; but lifting the thing
that keeps you anchored, and sailing out. Then gravita-
tion, in conjunction with what rightfully attracts you,
might be in an upward as well as a downward direction—or what we call up and down would cease to
signify. We crave only reality; but since "We know not
where we are" (XVIII, 16) and only "esteem truth remote" (II, 21)—that is, we cannot believe that it is
under our feet—we despair of ourselves and let our
despair dictate what we call reality: "When we consider
what, to use the words of the catechism, is the chief end
of man, and what are the true necessaries and means of
life, it appears as if men had deliberately chosen the
common mode of living because they preferred it to
any other. Yet they honestly think there is no choice
left" (I, 10). The way we live is not necessary, in this
"comparatively free country." The writer generally
"[confines himself] to those who are said to be in *moderate* circumstances" (I, 53), obviously implying that he
thinks their case is extreme. It follows that this life has
been chosen; that since we are living and pursuing it,
we are choosing it. This does not appear to those leading it to be the case; they think they haven't the means
to live any other way. "One young man of my acquaintance, who has inherited some acres, told me that he

thought he should live as I did, *if he had the means*" (I, 99). But the truth appears to the writer, as if in a vision, a vision of true necessities, that the necessaries of life *are* the means of life, the ways it is lived; therefore to say we haven't the means for a different way, in particular for a way which is to discover what the true necessaries and means of life in fact are, is irrational. It expresses the opinion that our current necessities are our final ones. We have defined our lives in front. What at first seems like a deliberate choice turns out to be a choice all right (they honestly think there is no choice *left*), but not a deliberate one, not one weighed and found good, but one taken without pondering, or lightly; they have never preferred it. And yet this is nothing less than a choice of one's life.

How does this come about? What keeps this nightmare from at least frightening us awake? It is a sort of disease of the imagination, both of the private imagination we may call religion and of the public imagination we may call politics. To settle, weigh, gravitate, he was saying, is a question of "taking the case that is," not "supposing a case." And earlier: "I am far from supposing that my case is a peculiar one; no doubt many of my readers would make a similar defense" (I, 102). That is, from our own experience we draw or project our definitions of reality, as the empiricists taught us to do; only the experience we learn from, and know best, is our failure (cf. II, 21), the same old prospects are repeated back to us, by ourselves and by others. We were to be freed from superstition; instead the frozen hopes and fears which attached to rumored dictates of revelation have now attached themselves to the rumored dictates of experience. The writer calls us heathenish.

(He calls himself that too because to an audience of heathens all devotions are heathenish; and because if what *they* do is called Christianity then he is a heathen — he lives outside the town.) Our education is sadly neglected; we have not learned in the moral life, as the scientists have in theirs, how to seek and press to the limits of experience; so we draw our limits well short of anything reason requires. The result is not that the reality this proposes to us, while confined, is at least safe. The result is a metaphysics of the imagination, of unexamined fantasy.

As I was desirous to recover the long lost bottom of Walden Pond, I surveyed it carefully, before the ice broke up, early in '46, with compass and chain and sounding line. There have been many stories told about the bottom, or rather no bottom of this pond, which certainly had no foundation for themselves. It is remarkable how long men will believe in the bottomlessness of a pond without taking the trouble to sound it. I have visited two such Bottomless Ponds in one walk in this neighborhood. Many have believed that Walden reached quite through to the other side of the globe. Some who have lain flat on the ice for a long time, looking down through the illusive medium, perchance with watery eyes into the bargain, and driven to hasty conclusions by the fear of catching cold in their breasts, have seen vast holes "into which a load of hay might be driven," if there were anybody to drive it, the undoubted source of the Styx and entrance to the Infernal Regions from these parts. Others have gone down from the village with a "fifty-six" and a wagon-load of inch rope, but yet have failed to find any bottom; for while the "fifty-six" was resting by the way, they were paying out the rope in the vain attempt to fathom their truly immeasurable capacity for marvelousness. But I can assure my readers that

Walden has a reasonably tight bottom at a not unreasonable, though at an unusual, depth. I fathomed it easily with a cod-line and a stone weighing about a pound and a half, and could tell accurately when the stone left the bottom, by having to pull so much harder before the water got underneath to help me. The greatest depth was exactly one hundred and two feet; to which may be added the five feet which it has risen since, making one hundred and seven. This is a remarkable depth for so small an area; yet not one inch of it can be spared by the imagination. What if all ponds were shallow? Would it not react on the minds of men? I am thankful that this pond was made deep and pure for a symbol. While men believe in the infinite some ponds will be thought to be bottomless. (xvi, 6)

The human imagination is released by fact. Alone, left to its own devices, it will not recover reality, it will not form an edge. So a favorite trust of the Romantics has, along with what we know of experience, to be brought under instruction; the one kept from straining, the other from stifling itself to death. Both imagination and experience continue to require what the Renaissance had in mind, viz., that they be humanized. ("I brag for humanity," i.e., the humanity that is still to awaken, to have its renascense. And the writer praises science that humanizes knowledge, that "reports what those men already know practically or instinctively," as "a true *humanity*, or account of experience" [xi, 1], i.e., one of the humanities.) The Reformation, as in Luther and Milton, had meant to be a furthering of this too. It was not wholly ineffective: "Our manners have been corrupted by communication with the saints" (i, 109). That is, false saintliness is hypocrisy, but true saintliness will seem to be bad manners to hypocrites.

The work of humanization is still to be done. While men believe in the infinite some ponds will be thought to be bottomless. So long as we will not take our beliefs all the way to genuine knowledge, to conviction, but keep letting ourselves be driven to more or less hasty conclusions, we will keep misplacing the infinite, and so grasp neither heaven nor earth. There is a solid bottom everywhere. But how are we going to weigh toward it, arrive at confident conclusions from which we can reverse direction, spring an arch, choose our lives, and go about our business?

Despair is not bottomless, merely endless; a hopelessness, or fear, of reaching bottom. It takes illusions for its object, from which, in turn, like all ill-educated experience, it is confirmed in what it already knew. So its conclusions too are somewhat hasty, its convictions do not truly convict us. This is a prophecy the writer hears from a cat with wings:

Suddenly an unmistakable cat-owl from very near me, with the most harsh and tremendous voice I ever heard from any inhabitant of the woods, responded at regular intervals to the [loud honking of a] goose, as if determined to expose and disgrace this intruder from Hudson's Bay by exhibiting a greater compass and volume of voice in a native, and *boo-hoo* him out of Concord horizon. What do you mean by alarming the citadel at this time of night consecrated to me? Do you think I am ever caught napping at such an hour, and that I have not got lungs and a larynx as well as yourself? *Boo-hoo, boo-hoo, boo-hoo!* It was one of the most thrilling discords I ever heard. And yet, if you had a discriminating ear, there were in it the elements of a concord such as these plains never saw nor heard. (xv, 2)

If we find out what is foreign and what is native to us, we can find out what there really is to boo-hoo about, and then our quiet wailing will make way for something to crow about.

What has the writer's ear discriminated specifically? Evidently he has heard that all the elements of an apocalyptic concord, a new city of man, are present. We need nothing more and need do nothing new in order that our change of direction take place. This is expressed in the writer's constant sense that we are on the verge of something, perched; something is in the wind, Olympus is but the outside of earth everywhere; there is a solid bottom everywhere; the dumps and a budding ecstasy are equally possible from this spot, we need only turn around to find the track. "Nearest to all things is that power which fashions their being. *Next* to us the grandest laws are continually being executed" (v, 6). Because we do not recognize the circumstances that encircle us, we do not allow them to "make our occasions"; instead of "looking another way" (ii, 22), we permit outlying and transient circumstances to distract us. The crisis is at hand, but we do not know how to grasp it; we do not know where or how to spend it, so we are desperate. But "it is characteristic of wisdom not to do desperate things" (i, 9). And "It is by a mathematical point only that we are wise, as the sailor or the fugitive slave keeps the polestar in his eye" (i, 99). The day is at hand, and the effect of every vision is at hand—for example, of renaissance and reformation and revolution (we are to work our way through poetry and philosophy and church and state), which since the beginning of the modern age have been a "dinning in our ears" (xviii, 9).

This is, no doubt, mystical to us. But the wretchedness and nervousness this writing creates come from an
equally undeniable, if intermittent, sense that the writer
is being practical, and therefore that we are not. It is a
sense that the mystery is of our own making; that it
would require no more expenditure of spirit and body
to let ourselves be free than it is costing us to keep
ourselves pinioned and imprisoned within "opinion,
and prejudice, and tradition, and delusion, and appearance." Our labors — the *way* we labor — are not responses to true need, but hectic efforts to keep ourselves from the knowledge of what is needful, from the
promise of freedom, whose tidings we always call glad
and whose bringer we always despise and then apotheo-
size (1, 54), which is to say, kick upstairs. It is no excuse
to us that few tidings really are glad, that for every real
prophet there are legions of false ones speaking a vision
of their own hearts, i.e., from what ails merely themselves. We are not excused from thinking it out for
ourselves.

This writer's primary audience is neither the "degraded rich" nor the "degraded poor," but those who
are in "*moderate* circumstances"; what we might call
the *middle* class. We are not Chinese or Sandwich Islanders; nor are we *southern* slaves. "I sometimes wonder that we can be so frivolous, I may almost say, as to
attend to the gross but somewhat foreign form of servitude called Negro Slavery, there are so many keen and
subtle masters that enslave both North and South" (1,
8). There is no mystery here; there is plain damnation.
One mystery we make for ourselves is to say that Negro
slavery is wholly foreign to us who are said to live in
New England. South is for us merely a direction in

which we look away from our own servitude. This is to recommend neither that we ought or ought not do something about Negro slavery; it is to ask why, if we will not attend to the matter, we attend to it—as if fascinated by something at once foreign and yet intimately familiar. We have not made the South foreign to us, we have not put it behind us, sloughed its slavery. We do not yet see our hand in it, any more than we see the connection between our making ourselves foreign to our government and the existence of roasting Mexicans and "strolling" Indians (I, 31) (it was in the years immediately after Thoreau's graduation from Harvard that the eastern tribes were collected and, following Andrew Jackson's legislation, marched beyond the Mississippi); any more than we see the connection between what we call philanthropy and what we call poverty. We have yet "*to get our living together*" (I, 100), to be whole, and to be one community. We are not settled, we have not clarified ourselves; our character, and the character of the nation, is not (in another of his favorite words) transparent to itself (IX, 34).

It is hard to have a Southern overseer; it is worse to have a Northern one; but worst of all when you are the slave-driver of yourself. Talk of a divinity in man! Look at the teamster on the highway, wending to market by day or night; does any divinity stir within him? His highest duty to fodder and water his horses! What is his destiny to him compared with the shipping interests? Does not he drive for Squire Make-a-stir: How godlike, how immortal, is he? See how he cowers and sneaks, how vaguely all the day he fears, not being immortal and divine, but the slave and prisoner of his own opinion of himself, a fame won by his own deeds. Public opinion is a weak tyrant compared with our own private opinion. What a man thinks of himself, that it is which determines, or rather indicates, his fate. Self-emancipation even in the West Indian provinces of the fancy and imagination — what Wilberforce is there to bring that about? Think, also, of the ladies of the land weaving toilet cushions against the last day, not to betray too green an interest in their fates! As if you could kill time without injuring eternity. (I, 8)

How did private opinion become a tyrant, a usurper, in service of interests not our own? Its power is such — not merely the magnitude of it, but the form of it — that we feel not merely helpless before it but without rights in the face of it. The drift of *Walden* is not that we should go off and be alone; the drift is that we *are* alone, *and* that we are never alone — not in the highest and not in the lowest sense. In the highest sense, we will know a good neighborhood when we can live there; and in the lowest, "Consider the girls in a factory — never alone, hardly in their dreams" (V, 13). In such circumstances there is little point in suggesting that we assert ourselves, or take further steps; that merely asks the tyrant to tighten his hold. The quest of this book is for the recovery of the self, as from an illness: "The incessant anxiety and strain of some is a well-nigh incurable form of disease" (I, 15).

Why should we explore ourselves when we already know ourselves for cowards, sneaks, and slaves? "But men labor under a mistake" (I, 5). Our labors are not callings, but neither are they misfortunes or accidents which have befallen us. In all, we take something for what it is not but, understandably enough, something it appears to be. That is the cause of our despair, but also cause for hope. We do not *know* that it is necessary for things to be as bad as they are; because we do not know why we labor as we do. We take one thing for another in every field of thought and in every mode of action. Religiously, our labors betoken penance, hence a belief in works without faith, hence blindness to faith; politically, our labors betoken a belief in fate, hence in a society whose necessities we have had no hand in determining, hence blindness to its origins; epistemologically, our labors betoken superstitions, commitments to uncertainties (i, 15), refusals to know what we know. ("Man flows at once to God when the channel of purity is open" [XI, 11].)

The writer knows his readers will take the project of self-emancipation to be merely literary. But he also knows that this is because they take everything in a more or less literary way: everything is news to them, and it always comes from foreign parts, from some Gothic setting. "Shams and delusions are esteemed for soundest truths, while reality is fabulous" (II, 21). We crave only reality, but we cannot stomach it; we do not believe in our lives, so we trade them for stories; their real history is more interesting than anything we now know.

How are we to become practical? How are we to "look another way," i.e., look in another way, with other eyes, in order to understand that it is harder to be "an overseer of the poor" (i, 109) (i.e., of ourselves) than to let ourselves go? All our fields await emancipation — geography and places, literature and neighborhood, epistemology and eyes, anatomy and hands, metaphysics and cities. To locate ourselves in this maze, the first step is to see that we ourselves are its

architects and hence are in a position to recollect the
design. The first step in building our dwelling is to
recognize that we have already built one.

Society remains as mysterious to us as we are to
ourselves, or as God is. That we are the slave-drivers of
ourselves has not come about "for private reasons, as
[we] must believe" (1, 10). It is an open realization of
what we have made of the prophecy of democracy. It is
what we have done with the success of Locke and the
others in removing the divine right of kings and placing
political authority in our consent to be governed together. That this has made life a little easier for some, in
some respects, is a less important consequence than the
fact that we now consent to social evil. What was to be a
blessing we have made a curse. We do not see our hand
in what happens, so we call certain events melancholy
accidents when they are the inevitabilities of our projects (1, 75), and we call other events necessities because
we will not change our minds. The essential message of
the idea of a social contract is that political institutions
require justification, that they are absolutely without
sanctity, that power over us is held on trust from us,
that institutions have no authority other than the authority we lend them, that we are their architects, that
they are therefore artifacts, that there are laws or ends,
of nature or justice, in terms of which they are to be
tested. They are experiments.

To learn that we have forgotten this is part of our
education which is sadly neglected.

We read that the traveler asked the boy if the swamp
before him had a hard bottom. The boy replied that it
had. But presently the traveler's horse sank in up to the
girths, and he observed to the boy, "I thought you said

> that this bog had a hard bottom." "So it has," answered
> the latter, "but you have not got half way to it yet." So it
> is with the bogs and quicksands of society; but he is an
> old boy that knows it. (XVIII, 14)

The bottom is our construction of it, our cursed consent to it, our obedience to it which we read as a muddle
of accidents and necessities. The writer suggests this in
saying that he "[desires] to speak impartially on this
point, and as one not interested in the success or failure
of the present economical and social arrangements" (1,
77). Since "not interested in" evidently cannot mean
that they have no interest for him, what does it mean? It
means that he is one who is withdrawing his interest in
it, placing his investment elsewhere. Or he "desires to
speak" as if that were so, leaving it open whether it is
the case. Not simply because he would make a fiction of
his withdrawal, but because it is unclear how it is to be
effected. This is in fact one of the standing mysteries of
any theory of the social contract—how consent is
shown, and therefore when and how its withdrawal can
be shown.

It is, appropriately, in the chapter gently entitled
"The Village" that the writer of *Walden* declares himself to be the author of "Civil Disobedience," the same
man who had said that "I simply wish to refuse allegiance to the State, to withdraw and stand aloof from it
effectually" (CD, 36). In that essay he describes himself
as having felt, during his one night in jail, a kind of
ecstasy of freedom. But that hardly constitutes "effec-
tual" withdrawal from the state. He reprints a statement he said he put in writing to the effect that he did
"not wish to be regarded as a member of any incorpo-
rated society which I have not joined." That seems to

have disengaged him from the local church; and though he would "have signed off in detail from all the societies which [he] never signed on to . . . [he] did not know where to find a complete list" (CD, 25). The joke very quickly went sour. In particular, he could not name society or the government as such, because he knows he has somehow signed on. "How does it become a man to behave toward this American government today? I answer, that he cannot without disgrace be associated with it. I cannot for an instant recognize that political organization as *my* government which is the *slave's* government also" (CD, 7). Nevertheless, he recognizes that he *is* associated with it, that his withdrawal has not "dissolved the Union" between ourselves and the state (cf. CD, 14), and hence that he is disgraced. Apparently, as things stand, one cannot but choose to serve the state; so he will "serve the state with [his conscience] also, and so necessarily resist it for the most part" (CD, 5). This is not a call to revolution, because that depends, as Locke had said, on supposing that your fellow citizens, in conscience, will also find that the time for it has come; and Thoreau recognizes that "almost all say that such is not the case now" (CD, 8).

Effective civil disobedience, according to Thoreau's essay, is an act that accomplishes three things: (1) it forces the state to recognize that you are against it, so that the state, as it were, attempts to withdraw your consent for you; (2) it enters an appeal to the people " . . . first and instantaneously, from them to the Maker of them, and, secondly, from them to themselves" (CD, 39), because the state has provided, in the given case, no other way of petition (CD, 19); (3) it identifies and educates those who have "voluntarily chosen to be an

agent of the government" (CD, 21). ("How shall he ever
know well what he is and does as an officer of the
government, or as a man, until he is obliged to consider
whether he shall treat me, his neighbor, for whom he
has respect, as a neighbor and well-disposed man, or as
a maniac and disturber of the peace, and see if he can
get over this obstruction to his neighborliness without a
ruder and more impetuous thought or speech corre-
sponding with his action" [CD, 21].) One night in jail
was not much in the way of such an action; in fact it
lacked the second condition of such an act altogether,
viz., the appeal to the people from themselves. But
those who complain of the pettiness of that one night
forget that the completion of the act was the writing of
the essay which depicts it.

Even that is likely to be as ineffective as a quiet night
in the Concord jail. First, because the state is "penitent
to that degree that it [will hire] one to scourge it while it
[sins], but not to that degree that it [will leave] off
sinning for a moment" (CD, 13); second, because an
appeal to the people will go unheard as long as they do
not know who they are, and labor under a mistake, and
cannot locate where they live and what they live for.
Nothing less than *Walden* could carry that load of information. Like the *Leviathan*, and the *Second Treatise of
Government*, and the *Discourse on the Origin of Inequal-
ity*—which we perhaps regard as more or less prescien-
tific studies of existing societies—*Walden* is, among
other things, a tract of political education, education
for membership in the polis. It locates authority in the
citizens and it identifies citizens—those with whom
one is in membership—as "neighbors." What it shows
is that education for citizenship is education for isola-

tion. (In this sense, *Walden* is *Émile* grown up. The absence of Sophie only purifies the point.)

The writer of *Walden* keeps faith both with his vision of injustice in his early essay, and with his strategy in the face of it: he resists society by visibly withdrawing from it. "It is true, I might have resisted forcibly with more or less effect, might have run 'amok' against society; but I preferred that society should run 'amok' against me, it being the desperate party" (VIII, 3). The writer's strategy, which enforces his position as neighbor, is to refuse society his voice, letting the desperate party run amok not merely eventually, but now, against his words, unable either to accept them or to leave them alone. And he reaffirms his earlier judgment that prisons are "the only [houses] in a slave State in which a free man can abide with honor" (CD, 22), by "caging" himself in the woods (II, 9), keeping alive the fact and the imagination of injustice, and inhabiting "the more free and honorable ground" on which to be found by "the fugitive slave, and the Mexican prisoner on parole, and the Indian come to plead the wrongs of his race" (CD, 22)—all of whom make their appearance to him at Walden. He went there to "repeople the woods" (XIV, 15); first, by being there; second, by imagining those who were there before; third, by anticipating those for whom he is preparing the ground, those who have come to these woods and must be renewed. And he demonstrates three captivities: that he is a prisoner of the state, as any man is whose government is native to him and is evil; that he is, like Saint Paul, a prisoner of Christ; and that we are held captive each by each and each by the others. These captivities show where we live and what we live for; and the source of strength, or the fulcrum, upon which we can change direction.

It is not the first time in our literature, and it will not be the last, in which society is viewed as a prison. As with Plato's cave, the path out is as arduous as the one the *Republic* requires of philosophers — and like the *Republic*, *Walden* is presided over by the sun, and begins with a stripping away of false necessities. Its opening visions of self-torture and of eternal labors and self-enslavement seem to me an enactment of the greatest opening line among our texts of social existence: "Man is born free, and everywhere he is in chains." What I take Rousseau to mean is that the *way* man is in bondage is comprehensible only of the creature who is, ontologically, free. Human societies, as we know them, could not exist except with each individual's choosing not to exercise freedom. To choose freedom would be to choose freedom for all (to make the will general); the alternative is that we choose partially, i.e., to further our privilege or party. The social contract is nowhere in existence, because we do not will it; therefore the undeniable bonds between us are secured by our obedience to agreements and compacts that are being made among ourselves as individuals acting privately and in secret, not among ourselves as citizens acting openly on behalf of the polis. The logic of our position is that we are conspirators. If this is false, it is paranoid; if it is not, we are crazy. I mention this not to argue for it, or even to justify this reading of Rousseau, but only to suggest a degree of intimacy between Rousseau's and Thoreau's understanding of society; and at the same time to keep in mind the question of insanity to which the writer of *Walden* recurs — or at any rate, the extremity and precariousness of mood in which he writes.

I do not wish to impose a political theory upon the text of *Walden*. On the contrary, if the guiding question of political theory is "Why ought I to obey the state?" then Thoreau's response can be said to reject the question and the subject. The state is not to be obeyed but, at best, to be abided. It is not to be listened to, but watched. Why ought I to abide the state? Because "it is a great evil to make a stir about it." A government, however, is capable of greater evil, "when its tyranny or its inefficiency are great and unendurable" (CD, 8). How do you know when this point has been reached? Here the concept of conscience arises, upon which secular, or anyway empiricist philosophy has come to grief: what can conscience be, other than some kind of feeling, of its essence private, a study for psychologists?—as though the "science," that is to say knowledge, that the word "conscience" emphasizes can at most register a lingering superstition. *Walden*, in its emphasis upon listening and answering, outlines an epistemology of conscience.

The opening visions of captivity and despair in *Walden* are traced full length in the language of the first chapter, the longest, which establishes the underlying vocabulary of the book as a whole. "Economy" turns into a nightmare maze of terms about money and possessions and work, each turning toward and joining the others. No summary of this chapter will capture the number of economic terms the writer sets in motion in it. There is profit and loss, rich and poor, cost and expense, borrow and pay, owe and own, business, commerce, enterprises, ventures, affairs, capital, price, amount, improvement, bargain, employment, inheritance, bankruptcy, work, trade, labor, idle, spend, waste, allowance, fortune, gain, earn, afford, possession, change, settling, living, interest, prospects, means, terms. But the mere listing of individual words gives no idea of the powers of affinity among them and their radiation into the remainder of language. They are all ordinary words that we may use, apparently literally, in evaluating any of our investments of feeling, or expenses of spirit, or turns of fortune. There is just enough description, in this chapter, of various enterprises we think of as the habitual and specific subjects of economics, to make unnoticeable the spillage of these words over our lives as a whole. It is a brutal mocking of our sense of values, by forcing a finger of the vocabulary of the New Testament (hence of our understanding of it) down our throats. For that is the obvious origin or locus of the use of economic imagery to express, and correct, spiritual confusion: what shall it profit a man; the wages of sin; the parable of talents; laying up treasures; rendering unto Caesar; charity. What we call the Protestant Ethic, the use of worldly loss and gain to symbolize heavenly standing, appears in *Walden* as some last suffocation of the soul. America and its Christianity have become perfect, dreamlike literalizations or parodies of themselves.

The network or medium of economic terms serves the writer as an imitation of the horizon and strength both of our assessments of our position and of our connections with one another; in particular of our eternal activity in these assessments and connections, and of our blindness to them, to the fact that they are ours. The state of our society and the state of our minds are stamped upon one another. This was Plato's metaphysical assumption in picturing justice and its decline; it was the secret of Rousseau's epistemology. To let light into this structure of terms, to show that our facts and ideas of economy are uneconomical, that they do not meet but avoid true need, that they are as unjust and impoverishing within each soul as they are throughout the soul's society, *Walden* cuts into the structure of economic terms at two major points, or in two major ways: (1) it attacks its show of practicality by dramatizing the mysteriousness of ownership, and (2) it slips its control of several key terms.

I do not claim that Locke is the only or even the actual representative of the mystery of ownership that *Walden* encounters. But the *Second Treatise* is as formative of the conscience, or the unconsciousness, of political economy as any other work, and its preoccupations are coded into *Walden*. When we read that "the cost of a thing is the amount of what I will call life which is required to be exchanged for it" (1, 45), it is inevitable that we should think of the so-called labor theory of value. The mysticism of what society thinks practical shows up nakedly in what anybody recognizes as the foolishness of Locke's justifications of ownership, in particular his idea that what originally entitles you to a thing is your having "mixed your labor" with it, and that what entitles you to more than you need is your "improvement" of the possession, your not wasting it. "Economy is a subject which admits of being treated with levity, but it cannot so be disposed of" (1, 44). The writer might at that point have had in mind Locke's argument that an individual's accumulation of vastly more money than he can spend is not a case of waste because money is metal and hence can be kept in heaps without being spoiled. The mysteries *Walden* goes into about buying and selling all the farms in his neighborhood, and about annually carrying off the landscape (II, 2), suggest that nobody really knows how it happens that anyone owns anything at all, or why it is that, as Locke puts it, though the earth was given to us in common, it is now so uncommonly divided and held. This is not to say that any of our institutions might not be practically justified (the writer of *Walden* describes and accepts a perfectly practical justification for the institution of money: that it is more convenient than barter). But in fact if you look at what we do under our pleas of economy, you see that no merely practical motives could inspire these labors.

Political economy is the modern form of theodicy, and our labors are our religious mysteries. This is an explicit meaning the writer gives, toward the end of "Economy," to his having spoken at its beginning of our "outward condition." He recounts an Indian custom described in Bartram, in which members of a community cleanse their houses and, having provided themselves with new clothes and utensils and furniture, throw the old together on a common heap, "consume it with fire," fast, and declare a "general amnesty" (I, 91). They are beginning again.

> The Mexicans also practiced a similar purification . . . in the belief that it was time for the world to come to an end . . .
> . . . I have scarcely heard of a truer sacrament, that is, as the dictionary defines it, "outward and visible sign of an inward and spiritual grace." (I, 94, 95)

So our labors, our outward condition, which he more than once describes as something to which we are "religiously devoted," are our sacraments, and the inward state they signal ("our very lives are our disgrace") is our secret belief that the world has already come to an end for us. Such actions are inspired, but not, as the writer says he believes in the case of the Mexicans, "directly from Heaven." We labor under a mistake. What will save us from ourselves is nothing less than salvation.

The second major strategy I said *Walden* uses to cut into the circling of economic terms is to win back from it possession of our words. This requires replacing them into a reconceived human existence. That it requires a literary redemption of language altogether has been a theme of my remarks from the beginning; and I have hoped to show that it simultaneously requires a redemption of the lives we live by them, religiously or politically conceived, inner and outer. Our words have for us the meaning we give to them. As our lives stand, the meaning we give them is rebuked by the meaning they have in our language—the meaning, say, that writers live on, the meaning we also, in moments, know they have but which mostly remains a mystery to us. Thoreau is doing with our ordinary assertions what Wittgenstein does with our more patently philosophical assertions—bringing them back to a context in which they are alive. It is the appeal from ordinary language to itself; a rebuke of our lives by what we may know of them, if we will. The writer has secrets to tell which can only be told to strangers. The secrets are not his, and they are not the confidences of others. They are secrets because few are anxious to know them; all but one or two wish to remain foreign. Only those who recognize themselves as strangers can be told them, because those who think themselves familiars will think they have already heard what the writer is saying. They will not understand his speaking in confidence.

The literary redemption of language is at the same time a philosophical redemption; the establishment of American literature undertaken in *Walden* requires not only the writing of a scripture and an epic, but a work of philosophy. The general reason is as before: *Walden* proposes new mysteries because we have already mystified ourselves; it requires new literary invention because we have already made our lives fabulous; it requires theology because we are theologized. We have already philosophized our lives almost beyond comprehension. The more famous perception of this is assumed in Marx's eleventh slogan concerning Feuerbach: "Philosophers have only interpreted the world in various ways; the point, however, is to change it." The changes required have to be directed to the fact that it is not only philosophers who have interpreted the world, but all men; that all men labor under a mistake—call it a false consciousness; and that those who learn true labor are going to be able to do something about this because they are the inheritors of philosophy, in a position to put philosophy's brags and hopes for humanity, its humanism, into practice. Why this is or is not going to happen now, and where, and how, are other matters. Who knows what our lives will be when we have shaken off the stupor of history, slipped the drag of time?

I have alluded to some of the literary-philosophical claims *Walden* stakes out for "owning," "improvement," "account," "interest," "living," and "loss." The announced subject in the opening chapter is the idea of a "necessary of life"; the most frequent among its characteristic signs is that of "necessity." It is from this term that I will begin to sketch what I have in mind when I think of this writing as a work of systematic philosophy — at least as a work which acknowledges the centrality, and perhaps the present impossibility, of such an enterprise.

The Transcendentalists, as Emerson in 1842 said, got their title from the philosophy of Kant. What it meant to them was something, one gathers, to the effect that man lives in two worlds, in one of which he is free, in the other determined; and that an Idea of Reason is an Idea to be aspired to. Emerson calls Transcendentalism the current flowering of idealism, contrasting that with a perennial materialism,

> the first class [materialists] founding on experience, the second [idealists] on consciousness; the first class beginning to think from the data of the senses, the second class perceive that the senses are not final, and say, The senses give us representations of things, but what are the things themselves, they cannot tell. . . . [The idealist] concedes all that the other affirms, admits the impressions of sense, admits their coherency, their use and beauty, and then asks the materialist for his grounds of assurance that things are as his senses represent them. But I, he says, affirm facts not affected by the illusions of sense. . . .

But because no one lives a perfectly spiritual existence, within the idealist "these two states of thought diverge every moment, in wild contrast. . . . The worst feature of this double consciousness is, that the two lives, of the understanding and of the soul, which we lead, really show little relation to one another." But the prevailing of the idea is his faith. "Patience is for us, is it not?"

The directly un-Kantian moment in Emerson's essay

is his notion that the senses are the scene of illusions. This at a stroke misconceives the undertaking of the *Critique of Pure Reason*, an essential half of which was exactly to answer, by transforming, the skeptical question about the existence of the external world, to show that things (as we know them) *are* as the senses represent them; that nature, the world opened to the senses, is objective. I am convinced that Thoreau had the Kantian idea right, that the objects of our knowledge require a transcendental (or we may say, grammatical or phenomenological) preparation; that we know just what meets the *a priori* conditions of our knowing anything *überhaupt*. These *a priori* conditions are necessities of human nature; and the search for them is something I think Thoreau's obsession with necessity is meant to declare. His difference from Kant on this point is that these *a priori* conditions are not themselves knowable *a priori*, but are to be discovered experimentally; historically, Hegel had said. *Walden* is also, accordingly, a response to skepticism, and not just in matters of knowledge. Epistemologically, its motive is the recovery of the object, in the form in which Kant left that problem and the German idealists and the Romantic poets picked it up, viz., a recovery of the thing-in-itself; in particular, of the relation between the subject of knowledge and its object. Morally, its motive is to answer, by transforming, the problem of the freedom of the will in the midst of a universe of natural laws, by which our conduct, like the rest of nature, is determined. *Walden*, in effect, provides a transcendental deduction for the concepts of the thing-in-itself and for determination—something Kant ought, so to speak, to have done.

What philosophers, men in thought, call the "determinism" of nature is in fact (i.e., really fits our concept of) fate. "By a seeming fate, commonly called necessity, [men] are employed, as it says in an old book, laying up treasures which moth and rust will corrupt" (i, 5). It is an idea of something controlled from beyond itself, toward a predetermined end or within predetermined confines. We did not get such an idea from nature, because what we find in nature is recurrence and "resolution" (xvi, 1); nature has no destiny beyond its presence; and it is completely autonomous, self-determined. So we must be projecting the idea into nature (it is an idea of reflection). Then the idea comes from our own sense of being controlled from outside. *Walden*'s concept for this is that of the *track*, and the most extended image of it is the new railroad.

> When I meet the engine with its train of cars moving off with planetary motion — or, rather, like a comet, for the beholder knows not if with that velocity and with that direction it will ever revisit this system, since its orbit does not look like a returning curve — with its steam cloud like a banner streaming behind in golden and silver wreaths, like many a downy cloud which I have seen, high in the heavens, unfolding its masses to the light — as if this traveling demigod, this cloud-compeller, would ere long take the sunset sky for the livery of his train; when I hear the iron horse make the hills echo with his snort like thunder, shaking the earth with his feet, and breathing fire and smoke from his nostrils (what kind of winged horse or fiery dragon they will put into the new Mythology I don't know), it seems as if the earth had got a race now worthy to inhabit it. If all were as it seems, and men made their elements their servants for noble ends! (iv, 8)

What happens instead is that men will mythologize their forces, as they always have, project them into demigods, and then serve their projections. Their latest heathenism was that of predestination and election ("I . . . would fain fancy myself one of the elect" [x, 2]); with the passing of that one, the new mythology will make the railroad engine (their technology, their inventions) their fate. It is, you might say, their inability to trust themselves to determine their lives; or rather, their inability to see that they are determining them. The world is what meets the conditions of what we call our necessities — whether we have really found them to be ours or not. "The universe constantly and obediently answers to our conceptions" (ii, 21). In particular, we have determined that we shall be governed by fate — by something that denies for us the incessant exercise of our control. "We have constructed a fate, an *Atropos*, that never turns aside" (iv, 10). The writer recommends that as the name of the engine in our new mythology.

What we have constructed is fate itself. That it never turns aside is merely what the word fate, or rather Atropos, means. And we are not fated to it; *we* can turn. We can learn a lesson from the railroad, as we can from the rest of what happens, if we can for once learn something that does not merely confirm our worst fears instead of our confidence.

> Men are advertised that at a certain hour and minute these bolts will be shot toward particular points of the compass; yet it interferes with no man's business, and the children go to school on the other track. We live the steadier for it. We are all educated thus to be sons of Tell.

The air is full of invisible bolts. Every path but your own
is the path of fate. Keep on your own track, then. (IV,
10)

"I too would fain be a track-repairer somewhere in the
orbit of the earth" (IV, 6). The lesson is that we can turn
from fate by keeping steady, keeping still. ("We have
the Saint Vitus' dance, and cannot possibly keep our
heads still" (II, 18); and of course the other way around
as well: as long as we do not learn to keep our heads
still, we will persist in the dance — as if to account for
our handicap. We must learn a "perpetual instilling"
[II, 21].) Your own is the path he calls wisdom, confidence, faith: "It is by a mathematical point only that we
are wise" (I, 99); one must advance "confidently in the
direction of [one's] dreams" (VXIII, 5). Everybody
more or less sees the sense of this. The question is how
we are to find this path, have the trust to accept it, since
everyone also more or less knows that it is an offer, a
promise. We live by fate because we are "determined
not to live by faith" (I, 15). Thus to determine ourselves requires constant vigilance and being on the
alert. But how do we stop determining ourselves? How
do we replace anxious wakefulness by a constant awakening?

Part of *Walden*'s answer we have already seen. We
have to learn what finding is, what it means that we are
looking for something we have lost. And we have to
learn what acceptance is, what it means that we have to
find ourselves where we are, at each present, and accept
that finding in our experiment, enter it in the account.
This is what requires confidence. To be confident of
nature, at every moment, appears as willingness to be

confided in by it. (" . . . I was surprised to hear him express wonder at any of Nature's operations, for I thought that there were no secrets between them" [XVII, 4].) This is why the writer's readings of nature do not feel like moralizations of it, but as though he is letting himself be read by it, confessed in it, listening to it, not talking about it. Finding and accepting and confidence and trust require our interest in our experiment, in our experiences, in what happens to us. Each of these concepts (finding, trust, interest, etc.) will exit into the others, and must be adjusted by the others.

What they come to is the learning of resolution. This is what will replace our determination, or commitment, to fate, to the absence of freedom. It is not a matter of doing something new, of determining a course of action and committing ourselves to it, as to jail (II, 5) or to an asylum. Resolution has to do with stillness and with settling (a "clearing," he sometimes calls it). The summary of the writer's learning this is told in his myth of winter, by what happens to him on the ice. It is there that he finds the bottom of the pond, and it is in winter that the owls prophesy and the fox awaits his transformation.

"The Pond in Winter" opens with the writer's depiction of himself awakening, enacting mythically the thing he is weaving his doctrine about.

> After a still winter night I awoke with the impression that some question had been put to me, which I had been endeavoring in vain to answer in my sleep, as what— how — when — where? But there was dawning Nature, in whom all creatures live, looking in at my windows . . . and no question on *her* lips. I awoke to an answered question, to Nature and daylight. . . . Nature puts no

question and answers none which we mortals ask. She
has long ago taken her resolution. (XVI, 1)

He awakes twice. First to the impression of a question
or questions which are the final recapitulation and placing of those questions with which his book begins.
They are very like those Christ alludes to in the Sermon
on the Mount: "Which of you by taking thought can
add one cubit unto his stature? . . . Therefore take no
thought, saying, What shall we eat? or, What shall we
drink? or Wherewithal shall we be clothed? . . . But
seek ye first the kingdom of God, and his righteous-
ness." That they have been asked while asleep — by
sleeping men to a man in a crisis of awakening — does
not mean they have no answers. His second waking is to
an answered question, i.e., to the fact that the questions have already been answered — or else that the
answer is in vain and the question, therefore, not understood. This is why he has to get us to ask, in order to
show that the answer is ours; we have given it, such as it
is. We may give another. That two wakings are required
he has indicated earlier, in "Reading":

> The at present unutterable things we may find some-
> where uttered. These same questions that disturb and
> puzzle and confound us have in their turn occurred to all
> the wise men; not one has been omitted; and each has
> answered them, according to his ability, by his words
> and his life. (III, 11)

Until the ice formed he had been answering by his
words; now he will answer in his life, show his definition. One answer we have seen: you have to lie on the
ice long enough not to settle upon hasty conclusions.

And other things happen to him out there. In search of water, "if that be not a dream" [he is still awakening], "I cut my way first through a foot of snow, and then a foot of ice, and open a window under my feet" — which means, against the book's preceding paragraph, that he is allowing himself to be looked in at. Kneeling there to drink he sees summer preserved in the sanded floor; recalling his earlier notice that heaven is reflected in Walden's water—it is "Sky water"—he now says, "Heaven is under our feet as well as over our heads" (XVI, 2). He has arrived at his location; and it is a kind of literalized Galilean answer to a question which earlier arose about the other side of the earth; people there are not upside down, because heaven is over their heads too, and under their feet. He has now "made some progress toward settling in the world" (II, 9), become "a track-repairer somewhere in the orbit of the earth," by realizing its planetary motion, surrounded by heaven. The locomotive seemed to have that motion when it suggested a race worthy to inhabit the earth; and it is his realization of "that farthest western way" he commends to us (XVIII, 2); for an earthling, diurnally, which is how it must happen, the direction to that way is eastward, i.e., toward dawn, increasingly.

The final event on the ice is this:

> Sometimes, also, when the ice was covered with shallow puddles, I saw a double shadow of myself, one standing on the head of the other, one on the ice, the other on the trees or hillside. (XVI, 15)

(He has added a cubit to his stature, and overcome himself. No doubt this is not the form in which we would have expected our doubleness to be projected.)

This is an ecstatic vision of something he predicted in the mystical harmonies and dissonances of "Solitude":

> With thinking we may be beside ourselves in a sane sense. By a conscious effort of the mind we can stand aloof from actions and their consequences. . . . We are not wholly involved in Nature. . . . I only know myself as a human entity; the scene, so to speak, of thoughts and affections; and am sensible of a certain doubleness by which I can stand as remote from myself as from another. However intense my experience, I am conscious of the presence and criticism of a part of me, which, as it were, is not a part of me, but a spectator, sharing no experience, but taking note of it, and that is no more I than it is you. (v, 11)

This is not Emerson's idea of an Over-Soul, most importantly because Emerson locates that, among other places, *within* the self, as a unity, or *the* Unity; and he leaves me the habitual spectator of my world. That is where Emerson is always stuck, with his sense, not his achievement, of outsideness, the yearning for the thing to happen to him. In "Solitude," it is the double who is the spectator, and I who am the scene of occurrence. The impersonality, or impartiality, of *Walden*'s double is the spiritual breakthrough from yearning and patience which releases its writer's capacity for action. It is a mode of what he calls "being interested in." It is the state, so far as I am able to estimate it, of the conclusion of *Oedipus at Colonus*, the absolute awareness of self without embarrassment — consciousness of self, and of the self's standing, beyond self-consciousness. ("When the play, it may be the tragedy, of life is over, the spectator goes his way" [v, 11].) Or it is the reflection in consciousness of what Freud meant by calling the greater part of us the Id. Philosophy has reflected it in the idea of a transcendental ego. *Walden* sometimes refers to it as imagination — when, for example, it remarks that "[the imagination and the body] should both sit down at the same table" (XI, 6). The name we find for the writer's description of the double does not at the moment matter; what is essential is that he gives his own view of what is apparently an ancient and recurring intimation of the wholeness of the self ("holiness groping for expression") out of a present sense of incoherence or division or incompleteness.

Our imagination, or our capacity for images, and for the meaning or phenomenology of our images — of dawn and day and night, of lower and higher, of straight and curved, hot and cold, freezing and melting and moulting, of birds and squirrels and snakes and frogs, of houses and bodies of water and words, of growth and decay, of mother and father — are as *a priori* as our other forms of knowledge of the world:

> When the ground was partially bare of snow, and a few warm days had dried its surface somewhat, it was pleasant to compare the first tender signs of the infant year just peeping forth with the stately beauty of the withered vegetation which had withstood the winter — life-everlasting, goldenrods, pinweeds, and graceful wild grasses, more obvious and interesting frequently than in summer even, as if their beauty was not ripe till then; even cotton-grass, cat-tails, mulleins, johnswort, hardhack, meadow-sweet, and other strong-stemmed plants, those unexhausted granaries which entertain the earliest birds — decent weeds, at least, which widowed Nature wears. I am particularly attracted by the arching and sheaflike top of the wool-grass; it brings back the sum-

mer to our winter memories, and is among the forms
which art loves to copy, and which, in the vegetable
kingdom, have the same relation to types already in the
mind of man that astronomy has. It is an antique style,
older than Greek or Egyptian. Many of the phenomena
of Winter are suggestive of an inexpressible tenderness
and fragile delicacy. We are accustomed to hear this king
described as a rude and boisterous tyrant; but with the
gentleness of a lover he adorns the tresses of Summer.
(XVII, 11)

Human forms of feeling, objects of human attraction,
our reactions constituted in art, are as universal and
necessary, as objective, as revelatory of the world, as
the forms of the laws of physics. This is the writer's
faith—confidence that what we are accustomed to call,
say, the "connotations" of words, the most evanescent
of the shadows they cast, are as available between us as
what we call their "denotations." That *in fact* we do not
normally avail ourselves of them is a comment on our
lives and shows our continuing need for art. (We have
yet to learn to *live* undefined in front.) This is another
way of seeing what I described as the writer's attempt to
register within the writing of the word the entire language from which a word is woven.

The writer specifies my relation to the double as my
being beside it. Being beside oneself is the dictionary
definition of ecstacy. To suggest that one may stand
there, stay there in a sane sense, is to suggest that the
besideness of which ecstasy speaks is my experience of
my existence, my knowledge "of myself as a human
entity," my assurance of my integrity or identity. This
condition—the condition of "having" a self, and
knowing it—is an instance of the general relation the
writer perceives as "being next to":

Any prospect of awakening or coming to life to a dead man makes indifferent all times and places. The place where that may occur is always the same, and indescribably pleasant to all our senses. For the most part we allow only outlying and transient circumstances to make our occasions. They are, in fact, the cause of our distraction. Nearest to all things is that power which fashions their being. *Next* to us the grandest laws are continually being executed. *Next* to us is not the workman whom we have hired, with whom we love so well to talk, but the workman whose work we are. (v, 6)

What is next to us is what we neighbor. The writer has spoken of finding himself suddenly neighbor to the birds; and he speaks of the pond in neighborly terms: "Of all the characters I have known, perhaps Walden wears best, and best preserves its purity" (ix, 25). Our relation to nature, at its best, would be that of neighboring it—knowing the grandest laws it is executing, while nevertheless "not wholly involved" in them.

> ... I experienced sometimes that the most sweet and tender, the most innocent and encouraging society may be found in any natural object.... I was suddenly sensible of such sweet and beneficent society in Nature ... an infinite and unaccountable friendliness all at once like an atmosphere sustaining me, as made the fancied advantages of human neighborhood insignificant, and I have never thought of them since. (v, 4)

(The idea that society is justified because it provides a set of "advantages"—an idea common to Locke's theory of a social contract and to Hume's criticism of that theory—is a fantasy. This of course does not mean that society's claims upon us are without authority.) You may call this mysticism, but it is a very particular view of the subject; it is not what the inexperienced may imagine as a claim to the union, or absorption in nature.*

As we are to learn the neighboring of nature so we are to learn the neighboring not of the workman whom we have hired (which is a measure of the kind of distance at which most people stand to themselves, slave-drivers of themselves, beside themselves in an insane sense) but of the workman whose work we are—which some may call God, and which is that in ourselves, or that aspect of ourselves, whom the writer calls the indweller:

> What of architectural beauty I now see, I know has gradually grown from within outward, out of the necessities and character of the indweller, who is the only builder—out of some unconscious truthfulness, and

* This is the place, but not the time, to try to make clearer what I mean by saying that *Walden* provides a transcendental deduction of the category of the thing-in-itself. I do not want to leave this claim without some explicit justification because it seems on the surface at best a play, at worst a contradiction in Kantian terms: the concept of the thing-in-itself is the result, if not exactly the conclusion, of Kant's idea of a transcendental deduction of the categories; it stands for the fact that knowledge has *limits*, or conditions. The concept, so to speak, just says that it has no transcendental deduction, that its object is not an object of knowledge for us, so to ask for a deduction of it is, on Kant's program, senseless. But what is "a thing which is not an object of knowledge for us"? Everyone involved with Kant's thought recognizes a problem here, the implication that there are things just like the things we know (or features of the very things we know) which, not answering to our conditions for knowing anything, are unknowable by us. We oughtn't to be able to attach any meaning at all to such an implication. If something does not answer to our conditions of knowledge then it is not subject to what we understand as knowledge, and that means that it is not what we understand as an object. A thing which we cannot know is not a thing. Then why are we led to speak otherwise? What is the sense that something escapes the conditions of knowledge? It is, I think, the sense, or fact, that our primary relation to the world is not one of knowing it (understood as

nobleness, without ever a thought for the appearance; and whatever additional beauty of this kind is destined to be produced will be preceded by a like and unconscious beauty of life. (1, 67)

And later:

> Every man is the builder of a temple, called his body, to the god he worships, after a style purely his own, nor can he get off by hammering marble instead. We are all sculptors and painters, and our material is our own flesh and blood and bones. Any nobleness begins at once to refine a man's features, any meanness or sensuality to imbrute them. (XI, 14)

Here are the elements of *Walden*'s solution to the problem of self-consciousness, or the sense of distance from self, or division of self. What *we* know as self-consciousness is only our opinion of ourselves, and like any other opinion it comes from outside; it is hearsay, our contribution to public opinion. We must become disobedient to it, resist it, no longer listen to it. We do that by keeping our senses still, listening another way, for

---

achieving certainty of it based upon the senses). This is the truth of skepticism. A Kantian "answer" to skepticism would be to accept its truth while denying the apparent implication that this is a *failure* of knowledge. This is the role the thing-in-itself ought, as it were, to have played. The idea of God is that of a relation in which the world as a whole stands; call it a relation of dependency, or of having something "beyond" it. The idea of the thing-in-itself is the idea of a relation in which we stand to the world as a whole; call it a relation of the world's externality (not each object's externality to every other — that is the idea of space; but the externality of all objects to us). When I said that Kant ought to have provided a deduction of the thing-in-itself, I meant that he had left unarticulated an essential feature (category) of objectivity itself, viz., that of *a world apart from me in which* objects are met. The externality of the world is articulated by Thoreau as its nextness to me.

something indescribably and unmistakably pleasant to all our senses. We are to reinterpret our sense of doubleness as a relation between ourselves in the aspect of indweller, unconsciously building, and in the aspect of spectator, impartially observing. Unity between these aspects is viewed not as a mutual absorption, but as a perpetual nextness, an act of neighboring or befriending. "This doubleness may easily make us poor neighbors and friends sometimes" (v, 11), because we have bestowed elsewhere our extent of trust and freeing and aid and comfort—or what looks to be elsewhere, given our current poor ideas of distance and nearness. (Our manners have been corrupted by communication with the saints.) The neighboring of the self is also articulated as the self's companionability: "I have a great deal of company in my house; especially in the morning, when nobody calls" (v, 15). When his imagination and his body sit down at the same table to eat they are etymologically companions. Society, if it is ever to better itself, depends upon each person's companionability; but, as things stand, society cannot teach this to us; it can merely impose something in its place. "We have had to agree on a certain set of rules, called etiquette and politeness, to make . . . frequent meeting tolerable and that we need not come to open war" (v, 13). No doubt it is better that it not come to that, but ontologically the state of society is nevertheless war—the condition which Hobbes claimed to be the state of nature. (Locke was enraged by Hobbes's claim, but he did not really correct it; nor did he provide a fuller or alternate account of what our relations in society are to be.) This is understood in Rousseau's insight that a philosopher's description of the state of nature is a projection of his own secret knowledge of the state of his society. *Wal-*

den's underlying notion, in its account of doubleness—
as opposed, say, to Plato's notion of the harmony of the
soul—is one of integrity conceived as an activity.

To maintain nextness to ourselves, we require new,
or newly conceived, capacities for constancy and for
change. These are invoked in *Walden*'s depiction of
resolution, which comprises both hardening and melting, the total concentration of resources and the total
expenditure of them; the suspension of winter and the
progression of spring. This resoluteness is not merely
an attitude one adopts in the face of others; that would
merely amount to unneighborliness, and would still
suggest that you were listening to the wrong thing. Our
position toward others should be an effect, not a cause,
of integrity. (Wordsworth, in "Resolution and Independence," apparently reverses this order: the poet
voices his resolve to independence after he comes upon
the old man. This may account for the anticlimax
which readers have felt in the explicit resolution contained in the poem's closing lines: " . . . I'll think of the
Leech-gatherer on the lonely moor!" But this is to
forget that the writing of the poem is the keeping of that
resolution, and that it is within the poem that the old
man appears, hence appears after the poet's resolution
has been taken.) Our first resolve should be toward the
nextness of the self to the self; it is the capacity not to
deny either of its positions or attitudes—that it is the
watchman or guardian of itself, and hence demands of
itself transparence, settling, clearing, constancy; and
that it is the workman, whose eye cannot see to the end
of its labors, but whose answerability is endless for the
constructions in which it houses itself. The answerability of the self to itself is its possibility of awakening.

Both the resolution of hardness and the resolution of

progression are matters of leaving, anticipations of departure. At the winter of one's crisis one relinquishes the world one has constructed and "dies down to the root" (XVII, 13); and "the root is faith" (I, 87). At the crisis of spring one forgoes that assurance in favor of the labors of rehabilitation. Each direction is an entrustment, or bequeathing, of the self.

I have come to the end of the questions I have wanted to pose about *Walden*. That I leave them incompletely explored will not matter if I have left them faithful and prompting enough for the book to take them out of my hands, to itself, for strangers. But there is a recurrent form of doubt about Thoreau's writing which may threaten the balance of any of my deliberations with his book and thereby take the heart out of the reader's efforts to try it further. The form of doubt is caused partly by the depth of the book's depressions and the height of its elevations, and, more nearly, by the absence of reconciliation between them, which may seem evasive or irresolute of the writer — as if we have been led once more only to the limits of one man's willingness to answer, not to the limits of the humanly answerable.

Does the writer of *Walden* really believe that the manner in which one conducts one's affairs can redeem their external meanness — that, for example, one could find one's Walden behind a bank counter, or driving a taxi, or guiding a trip hammer, or selling insurance, or teaching school? Granted that one is unlikely to find one's own Walden by roaming around the vicinity of Concord, Massachusetts, isn't it dishonest to suggest that it may be found in any place very different from that? Is it the way we live that he despises, or human life as such? Is it merely governments that he scorns, or the human need and capacity for human society altogether? Is it the way we treat our bodies that makes them ugly to him, or is he repelled by existence itself? Each of these questions has answers, too many answers; the voice wavers and swallows its words just when it seems that it should be surest of itself. I think Thoreau expresses this, and assumes his readers will also know these doubts. As before, barriers to the book are not tracings of its outworks but topics of its central soil.

There is to be found in this testament, as one would expect, a revelation in which the paradoxes and ambiguities of its doctrine achieve a visionary union. It does not exactly conclude the book, but threads through it. As typical of this writer's procedures, he acknowledges his relation to the Christian vision by overturning it, "revising" it. It is his way of continuing it. The threat of vision, as of any fantasy, lies in its partialness, its keeping half of its surface in the dark. The overcoming of fantasy is not its extirpation, but its revision, together with the revision of our lives, in favor of one another — telling the myth whole of which our visions are fragments.

The limiting revision of *Walden* concerns the fact that God's creation of the world has from the beginning gone wrong, or wanted completion. The writer of *Walden* proposes himself many times and in many ways as the creator of his world. "I have my horizon. . . . I have, as it were, my own sun and moon and stars, and a little world all to myself" (v, 3). The artist from Kouroo, whose condition he aspires to, "had made a new system in making a staff, a world with full and fair

proportions" (VXIII, 11). And beyond his acts of pub-
lishing nature, and repeopling the woods, assisting the
sun to rise (I, 25), giving the wind permission to howl
(XIII, 12), and floating the earth (II, 11), he is forever
"making a day of it" (II, 22; VII, 6). "To anticipate, not
the sunrise and the dawn merely, but, if possible,
Nature herself!" (I, 25)—that would mean to be in on
the beginning. This is not special about him. We *are*
creating the world, heaven is under our feet as well as
over our heads—however much of it we have placed.
The universe constantly and obediently answers to our
conceptions—whether they are mean or magnanimous, scientific or magical, faithful or treacherous.
Our choice is not between belief and unbelief, but
between faith and idolatry—whether we will be meta-
physicians or manikins. Specifically, the writer of *Walden* is as preoccupied as the writer of *Paradise Lost* with
the creation of a world by a word. (A word has meaning
against the context of a sentence. A sentence has meaning against the context of a language. A language has
meaning against the context of a form of life. A form of
life has meaning against the context of a world. A world
has meaning against the context of a word.) More specifically, the writer is preoccupied by the fact that the
creation of the world, whether in the *Old Testament* or
(say) in the *Vishnu Purana,* is a matter of *succession,* as
words are. The creation of the world is a creation of new
worlds, or new creations of the world. In the Wilson
translation of the *Vishnu Purana,* a favorite text of
Walden's writer:

> Whilst he [Brahma] formerly, in the beginning of the
> Kalpas, was meditating on creation, there appeared a
> creation beginning with ignorance, and consisting of
> darkness.... Brahma, beholding that it was defective,

designed another; and whilst he thus meditated, the
animal creation was manifested to the products of which
the term Tiryaksrotas is applied, from their nutriment
following a winding course. . . .

Beholding this creation also imperfect, Brahma again
meditated, and a third creation appeared, abounding
with the quality of goodness. . . . This, termed the creation of immortals, was the third performance of Brahma,
who, although well pleased with it, still found it incom-
petent to fulfil his end. Continuing therefore his meditations, there sprang . . . the creation termed Arvaksrotas
. . . from the downward current (of their nutriment).
They abound with the light of knowledge, but the qualities of darkness and of foulness predominate. Hence
they are afflicted by evil, and are repeatedly impelled to
action. They have knowledge both externally and inter-
nally, and are the instruments (of accomplishing the
object of creation, the liberation of soul). These creatures were mankind.

Apparently unlike the God of Genesis, Brahma does
not, after each day of creation, see that it is good. But
like Brahma, the God of Genesis requires time, fresh
days. The first day of creation is creation of the day,
giving time to himself—as though the author of nature
is also its editor, or commentator, as though responsibility to the vision is the capacity for revision. The first
reviser of mythology is God.

The winter visitor in whose company the writer kept
faith with God by revising mythology was "One of the
last of the philosophers—Connecticut gave him to the
world. . . . I think that he must be the man of the most
faith of any alive. . . . He is perhaps the sanest man and
has the fewest crotchets of any I chance to know" (XIV,
21). The writer marks this man, Bronson Alcott, as
"prompting God and disgracing man." Why does God

need prompting? Perhaps because the quarrel of man
and God has been an endless effort on each side to shift
to the other the burden of the world's revision. What
has God forgotten? What is he reluctant to do? In what
direction is the story which God began, or which begins
with God, to be revised? *Paradise Lost* spells out an
answer within Milton's faithfulness to the story:

> Know then, that after Lucifer from heaven
> (So call him, brighter once amidst the host
> Of angels than that star the stars among)
> Fell with his flaming legions through the deep
> Into his place, and the great Son returned
> Victorious with his saints, the omnipotent
> Eternal Father from his Throne beheld
> Their multitude, and to his Son thus spake: . . .
>
> . . . lest his heart exalt him in the harm
> Already done, to have dispeopled Heaven,
> My damage fondly deemed, I can repair
> That detriment, if such it be to lose
> Self-lost, and in a moment will create
> Another World, out of one man a race
> Of men innumerable, there to dwell,
> Not here, till by degrees of merit raised
> They open to themselves at length the way
> Up hither, under long obedience tried,
> And Earth be changed to Heaven, and Heaven to Earth,
> One kingdom, joy and union without end.

("Whichever way we turned, it seemed that the heav-
ens and the earth had met together, since he enhanced
the beauty of the landscape" [XIV, 21].)

To repeople heaven and earth we have to go back to
beginnings. In the beginning God meditated and the

heaven and the earth were created. There was a war in heaven which God was forced to win by meditating hell. The meditation of man is made in the midst of these divisions. We must prompt another meditation (we may all one day become meditators, students). We are to settle and work and wedge down "below freshet and frost and fire." Below fire there is ice, as in Dante's meditation. To melt that ice, allowing its prisoner to moult, is to undergo spring, in which earth and the first man are made again, of one another. But first we must undergo winter. We must follow the Word to the underworld; this time it will descend not as hell's conqueror but as its redeemer. Lucifer is Satan only in hell. He is in us, in our awaiting transformation (the foxes were barking raggedly and demoniacally); but we expel him, more or less, instead of transforming ourselves. He is in our labors and hopes (the locomotive breathes fire and smoke, and it awakens the writer) and in our unrested imaginations (which see entrances into the Infernal Regions from the bottom of the pond). To reverse direction, keeping on our true course, is still to pass through the center of gravity ("I love to weigh, to settle, to gravitate"). The brightness of Lucifer is our detraction from Christ. As we stand, in *Walden*'s last sentence, "The sun is but a morning star"; it reaches only a certain height and then declines. In Revelation the Son said that he will come as the bright and morning star, and that to him that overcometh he will give the morning star. The morning star is also, as in the meditation of Milton, Lucifer. The identity of Christ and Lucifer either is a curse, as in our lives as we lead them, or else it will eventually preside over our transformation. We dead will awaken not upon judgment, but because the day of judgment will be forgone, in favor of dawning. Until then, no fresh news will reach us. Thor must give way to Thaw (XVII, 10); so must Thoreau.

Leaving *Walden*, like leaving Walden, is as hard, is perhaps the same, as entering it. I have implied that the time of crisis depicted in this book is not alone a private one, and not wholly cosmic. It is simultaneously a crisis in the nation's life. And the nation too must die down to the root if it is to continue to recognize and neighbor itself. This is to be expected of a people whose groping for expression produced a literature by producing prophecy. They have had the strength to warn themselves. The hero of the book—as is typical of his procedures—enacts this fact as well as writes it, depicts it in his actions as well as his sentences. Of course the central action of building his house is the general prophecy: the nation, and the nation's people, have yet to be well made. And that the day is at hand for it to depart from its present constructions is amply shown in its hero's beginning and ending his tale with departures from Walden.

Two other of his actions specifically declare the sense of leaving or relinquishing as our present business. On the morning the writer went to dismantle the shanty he had bought as materials for his dwelling, and cart them to his new site, his labors were watched by one neighbor Seeley, who was taking the opportunity, as the writer was "treacherously informed," to steal what good nails, staples, and spikes the shanty yielded. "He was there to represent spectatordom, and help make this seemingly insignificant event one with the removal of the gods of Troy" (1, 63). Again, a classical myth shields a myth closer to home:

> Son of man, thou dwellest in the midst of a rebellious house, which have eyes to see, and see not; they have ears to hear, and hear not: for they are a rebellious house.
>
> Therefore, thou son of man, prepare thee stuff for removing, and remove by day in their sight; and thou shalt remove from thy place to another place in their sight: it may be they will consider, though they be a rebellious house. (Ezekiel 12:2–3)

The next step, if they do not consider, will be to go forth as into captivity. The writer's next step, accordingly, will be to return to civilization. The present constitution of our lives cannot go on. "This people must cease to hold slaves . . . though it cost them their existence as a people" (CD, 9). I do not quite wish to claim that Thoreau anticipated the Civil War; and yet the *Bhagavad Gita* is present in Walden—in name, and in moments of doctrine and structure. Its doctrine of "unattachment," so far as I am able to make that out, is recorded in *Walden*'s concept of interestedness. (This is, to my mind, one of Thoreau's best strokes. It suggests why "disinterestedness" has never really stabilized itself as a word meaning a state of impartial or unselfish interest, but keeps veering toward meaning the divestment of interest altogether, uninterestedness, ennui. Interestedness is already a state—perhaps the basic state—of relatedness to something beyond the self, the capacity for concern, for implication. It may be thought of as the self's capacity to mediate, to stand, between itself and the world.) Like *Walden*, the *Bhag-*

avad Gita is a scripture in eighteen parts; it begins with its hero in despair at the action before him; and it ends with his understanding and achieving of resolution, in particular his understanding of the doctrine (in which the image of the field and the knower of the field is central) that the way of knowledge and the way of work are one and the same, which permits him to take up the action it is his to perform and lead his army against an army of his kindred.

The second leaving, or relinquishment, is this:

> Now the trunks of trees on the bottom, and the old log canoe, and the dark surrounding woods, are gone, and the villagers, who scarcely know where it lies, instead of going to the pond to bathe or drink, are thinking to bring its water, which should be as sacred as the Ganges at least, to the village in a pipe, to wash their dishes with! — to earn their Walden by the turning of a cock or drawing of a plug! That devlish Iron Horse, whose ear-rending neigh is heard throughout the town, has muddied the Boiling Spring with his foot, and he it is that has browsed off all the woods on Walden shore. . . .

> . . . Though the woodchoppers have laid bare first this shore and then that, and the Irish have built their sties by it, and the railroad has infringed on its border, and the icemen have skimmed it once, it is itself unchanged, the same water which my youthful eyes fell on; all the change is in me. . . . It struck me again tonight, as if I had not seen it almost daily for more than twenty years— Why, here is Walden, the same woodland lake that I discovered so many years ago; where a forest was cut down last winter another is springing up by its shore as lustily as ever; the same thought is welling up to its surface that was then; it is the same liquid joy and happiness to itself and its Maker, ay, and it *may* be to me.

It is the work of a brave man surely, in whom there was
no guile! He rounded this water with his hand, deepened
and clarified it in his thought, and in his will bequeathed
it to Concord. I see by its face that it is visited by the
same reflection; and I can almost say, Walden, is it you?
(IX, 24, 25)

Walden was always gone, from the beginning of the
words of *Walden*. (*Our* nostalgia is as dull as our confidence and anticipation.) The first man and woman are
no longer there; our first relation to the world is no
longer secured by the world. To allow the world to
change, and to learn change from it, to permit it strangers, accepting its own strangeness, are conditions of
knowing it now. This is why its knowledge is a heroic
enterprise. The hero departs from his hut and goes into
an unknown wood from whose mysteries he wins a
boon that he brings back to his neighbors. The boon of
Walden is *Walden*. Its writer cups it in his hand, sees his
reflection in it, and holds it out to us. It is his promise,
in anticipation of his going, and the nation's, and Walden's. He is bequeathing it to us in his will, the place of
the book and the book of the place. He leaves us in one
another's keeping.

Thinking of Emerson

Thinking of Emerson

[INTRODUCTORY NOTE: For a program arranged by the Division on Philosophical Approaches to Literature at the annual convention of the Modern Language Association in New York, December 1978, Professor Leo Marx invented and chaired a meeting on Emerson whose panelists were asked by him to respond to a passage from my book *The Senses of Walden* that runs this way:

Study of *Walden* would perhaps not have become such an obsession with me had it not presented itself as a response to questions with which I was already obsessed: Why has America never expressed itself philosophically? Or has it — in the metaphysical riot of its greatest literature? Has the impulse to philosophical speculation been absorbed, or exhausted, by speculation in territory, as in such thoughts as Manifest Destiny? Or are such questions not really intelligible? They are, at any rate, disturbingly like the questions that were asked about American literature before it established itself. In rereading *Walden*, twenty years after first reading it, I seemed to find a book of sufficient intellectual scope and consistency to have established or inspired a tradition of thinking.

My response is the following essay, not quite all of which was read at the meeting. I am grateful to Leo Marx for prompting me to go further with these thoughts, and to Jay Cantor for reading the original draft and pressing me for certain clarifications. A conversation with John McNees was decisive for me in arriving at certain formulations about philosophical prose in its relation to the idea of dialogue and hence to an idea of thinking. I should in this regard also like to refer to an essay by Morse Peckham which appears as the introduction to a facsimile edition of the first printing of Emerson's *Essays* and *Essays: Second Series* (Columbus, 1969). I dedicate the present essay to the members, in the fall of 1978, of a graduate seminar at Harvard on the later writings of Heidegger.]

Thinking of Emerson, I can understand my book on *Walden* as something of an embarrassment, but something of an encouragement as well, since if what it suggests about the lack of a tradition of thinking in America is right, e.g., about how Emerson and Thoreau deaden one another's words, then my concentration on understanding Thoreau was bound to leave Emerson out. He kept sounding to me like secondhand Thoreau.

The most significant shortcoming among the places

my book mentions Emerson is its accusing him of "misconceiving" Kant's critical enterprise, comparing Emerson unfavorably in this regard with Thoreau. I had been impressed by Thoreau's sentence running "The universe constantly and obediently answers to our conceptions" as in effect an elegant summary of the *Critique of Pure Reason*. When I requote that sentence later in the book, I take it beyond its Kantian precincts, adding that the universe answers whether our conceptions are mean or magnanimous, scientific or magical, faithful or treacherous, thus suggesting that there are more ways of making a habitable world — or more layers to it — than Kant's twelve concepts of the understanding accommodate. But I make no effort to justify this idea of a "world" beyond claiming implicitly that as I used the word I was making sense. The idea is roughly that moods must be taken as having at least as sound a role in advising us of reality as sense-experience has; that, for example, coloring the world, attributing to it the qualities "mean" or "magnanimous," may be no less objective or subjective than coloring an apple, attributing to it the colors red or green. Or perhaps we should say: sense-experience is to objects what moods are to the world. The only philosopher I knew who had made an effort to formulate a kind of epistemology of moods, to find their revelations of what we call the world as sure as the revelations of what we call understanding, was the Heidegger of *Being and Time*. But it was hard to claim support there without committing oneself to more machinery than one had any business for.

Now I see that I might, even ought to, have seen Emerson ahead of me, since, for example, his essay on

"Experience" is about the epistemology, or say the logic, of moods. I understand the moral of that essay as contained in its late prayerful remark, "But far be from me the despair which prejudges the law by a paltry empiricism." That is, what is wrong with empiricism is not its reliance on experience but its paltry idea of experience. (This is the kind of criticism of classical empiricism leveled by John Dewey—for example, in "An Empirical Survey of Empiricisms"—who praised Emerson but so far as I know never took him up philosophically.) But I hear Kant working throughout Emerson's essay on "Experience," with his formulation of the question, "Is metaphysics possible?" and his line of answer: Genuine knowledge of (what we call) the world is for us, but it cannot extend beyond (what we call) experience. To which I take Emerson to be replying: Well and good, but then you had better be very careful what it is you understand by experience, for that might be limited in advance by the conceptual limitations you impose upon it, limited by what we know of human existence, i.e., by our limited experience of it. When, for example, you get around to telling us what we may hope for, I must know that you have experienced hope, or else I will surmise that you have not, which is to say precisely that your experience is of despair.

Emerson's "Experience" even contains a little argument, a little more explicitly with Kant, about the nature of experience in its relation to, or revelation of, the natural world. "The secret of the illusoriness [of life] is in the necessity of a succession of moods or objects. Gladly we would anchor, but the anchorage is quicksand. This onward trick of nature is too strong for us: *Pero si muove.*" In the section of the *Critique of Pure Reason* entitled "Analogies of Experience," one of the last before turning to an investigation of transcendental illusion, Kant is at pains to distinguish within experience the *"subjective succession* of apprehension from the *objective succession* of appearances." The anchor he uses to keep subjectivity and objectivity from sinking one another is, as you would expect, gripped in transcendental ground, which is always, for Kant, a question of locating necessity properly, in this case the necessity, or rules, of succession in experience. (It is curious, speaking of anchoring, that one of Kant's two examples in this specific regard is that of seeing a ship move downstream.) The acceptance of Galileo's—and Western science's—chilling crisis with the Church over the motion of the earth recalls Kant's claim to have accomplished a Copernican Revolution in metaphysics; that is, understanding the configurations of the world as a function of the configurations of our own nature. Now I construe Emerson's implicit argument in the passage cited as follows. The succession of moods is not tractable by the distinction between subjectivity and objectivity Kant proposes for experience. *This* onward trick of nature is too much for us; the given bases of the self are quicksand. The fact that we are taken over by this succession, this onwardness, means that you can think of it as at once a succession of moods (inner matters) and a succession of objects (outer matters). This very evanescence of the world proves its existence to me; it *is* what vanishes from me. I guess this is not realism exactly; but it is not solipsism either.

I believe Emerson may encourage the idea of himself as a solipsist or subjectivist, for example, in such a remark, late in the same essay, as "Thus inevitably does the universe wear our color." But whether you take this to be subjective or objective depends upon whether you take the successive colors or moods of the universe to be subjective or objective. My claim is that Emerson is out to destroy the ground on which such a problem takes itself seriously, I mean interprets itself as a metaphysical fixture. The universe is as separate from me, but as intimately part of me, as one on whose behalf I contest, and who therefore wears my color. We are in a state of "romance" with the universe (to use a word from the last sentence of the essay); we do not possess it, but our life is to return to it, in ever-widening circles, "onward and onward," but with as directed a goal as any quest can have; in the present case, until "the soul attains her due sphericity." Until then, encircled, straitened, you can say the soul is solipsistic; surely it is, to use another critical term of Emerson's, partial. This no doubt implies that we do not have a universe as it is in itself. But this implication is nothing: we do not have selves in themselves either. The universe *is* what constantly and obediently answers to our conceptions. It is what *can* be all the ways we know it to be, which is to say, all the ways we can be. In "Circles" we are told: "Whilst the eternal generation of circles proceeds, the eternal generator abides. That central life . . . contains all its circles." The universe contains all the colors it wears. That it has no more than I can give it is a fact of what Emerson calls my poverty. (Other philosophers may speak of the emptiness of the self.)

The Kantian ring of the idea of the universe as inevitably wearing our color is, notwithstanding, pertinent. Its implication is that the way specifically Kant understands the generation of the universe keeps it solipsistic, still something partial, something of our, of my, making. Emerson's most explicit reversal of Kant lies in his picturing the intellectual hemisphere of knowledge as passive or receptive and the intuitive or instinctual hemisphere as active or spontaneous. Whereas for Kant the basis of the *Critique of Pure Reason* is that "concepts are based on the spontaneity of thought, sensible intuitions on the receptivity of impressions." Briefly, there is no intellectual intuition. I will come back to this.

But immediately, to imagine that Emerson could challenge the basis of the argument of the *Critique of Pure Reason*, I would have to imagine him to be a philosopher — would I not? I would have, that is to say, to imagine his writing — to take it — in such a way that it does not misconceive Kant but undertakes to engage him in dispute. I like what Matthew Arnold has to say about Emerson, but we ought no longer to be as sure as Arnold was that the great philosophical writer is one who builds a system; hence that Emerson is not such a writer on the ground that he was not such a builder. We are by now too aware of the philosophical *attacks* on system or theory to place the emphasis in defining philosophy on a product of philosophy rather than on the process of philosophizing. We are more prepared to understand as philosophy a mode of thought that undertakes to bring philosophy to an end, as, say, Nietzsche and Wittgenstein attempt to do, not to mention, in their various ways, Bacon, Montaigne, Descartes, Pascal, Marx, Kierkegaard, Carnap, Heidegger, or Austin, and in certain respects Kant and Hegel. Ending philosophy looks to be a commitment of each of the

major modern philosophers; so it is hardly to be won-
dered at that some of them do not quite know whether
what they are writing is philosophy. Wittgenstein said
that what he did replaced philosophy. Heidegger said in
his later period that what he was doing was thinking, or
learning thinking, and that philosophy is the greatest
enemy of true thinking. But to understand the attack
on philosophy as itself philosophy, or undertaken in the
name, or rather in the place, of philosophy, we must of
course understand the attack as nevertheless internal to
the act of philosophizing, accepting that autonomy.
Church and State and the Academy and Poetry and the
City may each suppress philosophy, but they cannot,
without its complicity, replace it.

Can Emerson be understood as wishing to replace
philosophy? But isn't that wish really what accounts for
the poignancy, or dialectic, of Emerson's call, the year
Thoreau graduated college, not for a thinker but for
Man Thinking? The American Scholar is to think no
longer partially, as a man following a task delegated by a
society of which he is a victim, but as leading a life in
which thinking is of the essence, as a man whose wholeness, say whose autonomy, is in command of the autonomy of thinking. The hitch of course is that there is no
such human being. "Man in history, men in the world
today are bugs, spawn" ("The American Scholar").
But the catch is that we aspire to this man, to the
metamorphosis, to the human—hence that we can be
guided and raised by the cheer of thinking. In claiming
the office of the scholar "to cheer, to raise, and to guide
men" as well as demanding that "whatsoever new ver-
dict Reason from her inviolable seat pronounces on the
passing men and events of today—this [the scholar]

shall hear and promulgate," Emerson evidently requires the replacing of theology as well as of philosophy in his kind of building, his edification. We might think of this as internalizing the unended quarrel between philosophy and theology.

Whatever ways I go on to develop such thoughts are bound to be affected by the coincidence that during the months in which I was trying to get Emerson's tune into my ear, free of Thoreau's, I was also beginning to study the writing of the later Heidegger. This study was precipitated at last by a footnote of the editor of a collection of Heidegger essays, in which *The Senses of Walden* is described as in part forming an explication of Heidegger's notion of poetic dwelling (James G. Hart, in *The Piety of Thinking*). Having now read such an essay of Heidegger's as "Building Dwelling Thinking," I am sufficiently startled by the similarities to find the differences of interest and to start wondering about an account of both. I am thinking not so much of my similarities with Heidegger (I had after all profited from *Being and Time*, and it may be that that book leads more naturally to Heidegger's later work than is, I gather, sometimes supposed) but of Heidegger's with Thoreau, at least with my picture of Thoreau. The relation to Emerson was still unexpected, and hence even more startling. The title of the Heidegger collection I referred to is from a sentence of his that says: "For questioning is the piety of thinking." In the right mood, if you lay beside this a sentence of Emerson's from "Intellect" that says, "Always our thinking is a pious reception," you might well pause a moment. And if one starts digging to test how deep the connection might run, I find that one can become quite alarmed.

The principal text of Heidegger's to test here is translated as *What Is Called Thinking?* Here is a work that can be said to internalize the quarrel between philosophy and theology; that calls for a new existence from the human in relation to Being in order that its task of thinking be accomplished; a work based on the poignancy, or dialectic, of thinking about our having not yet learned true thinking, thinking as the receiving or letting be of something, as opposed to the positing or putting together of something, as this is pictured most systematically in Kant's ideas of representation and synthesis, and most radically in Nietzsche's will to power; that attempts to draw clear of Kant's subjectivity, and of the revenge upon time that Nietzsche understood us as taking. A climactic moment in Heidegger's descent into the origins of words is his understanding of the etymological entwining of thinking with the word for thanking, leading for example to an unfolding of ideas in which a certain progress of thinking is understood as a form of thanking, and originally a thanking for the gift of thinking, which means for the reception of being human. Here, if one can consider this to be something like philosophy, is something like a philosophical site within which to explore the crux in our relation to Emerson of his power of affirmation, or of his weakness for it.

We have surely known, since at least Newton Arvin (in "The House of Pain") collected the chorus of charges against Emerson to the effect that he lacked a knowledge of evil or of the sense of the tragic, that this missed Emerson's drift, that his task was elsewhere. Arvin insists, appropriately, that what Emerson gives us, what inspires us in him, "when we have cleared our minds of the cant of pessimism, is perhaps the fullest

and most authentic expression in modern literature of
the more-than-tragic emotion of thankfulness" (*Emerson: A Collection of Critical Essays,* ed. Konvitz and
Whicher). But we might have surmised from Nietzsche's love of Emerson that no sane or mere man could
have convincingly conceived "all things [to be] friendly
and sacred, all events holy, all men divine" who was not
aware that we may be undone by the pain of the world
we make and may not make again. The more recent
cant of pleasure or playfulness is no less hard to put up
with. Yet a more-than-tragic emotion of thankfulness is
still not the drift, or not the point. The point is the
achievement not of affirmation but of what Emerson
calls "the sacred affirmative" ("The Preacher"), the
thing Nietzsche calls "the sacred Yes" ("Three Metamorphoses" in *Zarathustra*), the heart for a new creation.
This is not an effort to move beyond tragedy — this has
taken care of itself; but to move beyond nihilism, or
beyond the curse of the charge of human depravity and
its consequent condemnation of us to despair; a charge
which is itself, Emerson in effect declares, the only
depravity ("New England Reformers").

(I may interject here that the idea of thinking as
reception, which began this path of reasoning, seems to
me to be a sound intuition, specifically to forward the
correct answer to skepticism [which Emerson meant it
to do]. The answer does not consist in denying the
conclusion of skepticism but in reconceiving its truth.
It is true that we do not know the existence of the world
with certainty; our relation to its existence is deeper —
one in which it is accepted, that is to say, received. My
favorite way of putting this is to say that existence is to
be acknowledged.)

So the similarity of Emerson with Heidegger can be

seen as mediated by Nietzsche; and this will raise more questions than it can answer. As to the question of what may look like the direction of influence, I am not claiming that Heidegger authenticates the thinking of Emerson and Thoreau; the contrary is, for me, fully as true, that Emerson and Thoreau may authorize our interest in Heidegger. Then further questions will concern the relation of the thinking of each of these writers to their respective traditions of poetry. To the figure of Hölderlin, Heidegger is indebted not alone for lessons of thought but for lessons in reading, and I suppose for the lesson that these are not different, or rather that there is ground upon which thinking and reading and philosophy and poetry meet and part. Emerson's implication in the history of the major line of American poetry is something that Harold Bloom has most concretely and I dare say most unforgettably given to us to think through. Emerson's and Thoreau's relation to poetry is inherently their interest in their own writing; they are their own Hölderlins. I do not mean their interest in what we may call their poems, but their interest in the fact that what they are building is writing, that their writing is, as it realizes itself daily under their hands, sentence by shunning sentence, the accomplishment of inhabitation, the making of it happen, the poetry of it. Their prose is a battle, using a remark of Nietzsche's, not to become poetry; a battle specifically to remain in conversation with itself, answerable to itself. (So they do write dialogues, and not monologues, after all.)

Such writing takes the same mode of relating to itself as reading and thinking do, the mode of the self's relation to itself, call it self-reliance. Then whatever is

required in possessing a self will be required in thinking and reading and writing. This possessing is not — it
is the reverse of — possessive; I have implied that in
being an act of creation, it is the exercise not of power
but of reception. Then the question is: On what terms
is the self received?

The answer I give for Emerson here is a theme of his
thinking that further stands it with the later Heidegger's, the thing Emerson calls "onward thinking," the
thing Heidegger means in taking thinking as a matter
essentially of getting ourselves "on the way."

At the beginning of "Circles" Emerson tells us he
means (having already deduced one moral in considering the circular or compensatory character of every human action) to trace a further analogy (or, read a further
sense; or, deduce a further moral) from the emblem of
the form of a circle. Since the time of "The American
Scholar" he has told us that "science is nothing but the
finding of analogy," and this seems a fair enough idea of
thinking. In "Circles" he invites us to think about the
fact, or what the fact symbolizes, that every action
admits of being outdone, that around every circle another circle can take its place. I should like to extend
the invitation to think about how he pictures us as
moving from one circle to another, something he sometimes thinks of as expanding, sometimes as rising. I
note that there is an ambiguity in his thoughts here as
between what he calls the *generating* and what he calls
the *drawing* of the new circle, an ambiguity between the
picturing of new circles as forming continuously or
discontinuously. I will not try to resolve this ambiguity
now but I will take it that the essential way of envision-
ing our growth, from the inside, is as discontinuous.

Then my questions are: How does Emerson picture us as crossing, or rather leaping, the span from one circumference to another? What is the motive, the means of motion, of this movement? How do we go on? (In Wittgenstein's *Philosophical Investigations*, knowing how to go on, as well as knowing when to stop, is exactly the measure of our knowing, or learning, in certain of its main regions or modes — for example, in the knowledge we have of our words. Onward thinking, on the way, knowing how to go on, are of course inflections or images of the religious idea of The Way, inflections which specifically deny that there is a place at which our ways end. Were philosophy to concede such a place, one knowable in advance of its setting out, philosophy would cede its own autonomy.)

You may imagine the answer to the question how we move as having to do with power. But power seems to be the result of rising, not the cause. ("Every new prospect is power" ["Circles"].) I take Emerson's answer to be what he means by "abandonment" (ibid.). The idea of abandonment contains what the preacher in Emerson calls "enthusiasm" or the New Englander in him calls "forgetting ourselves" (ibid.), together with what he calls leaving or relief or quitting or release or shunning or allowing or deliverance, which is freedom (as in "Leave your theory as Joseph his coat in the hand of the harlot, and flee" ["Self-Reliance"]), together further with something he means by trusting or suffering (as in the image of the traveler — the conscious intellect, the intellect alone —"who has lost his way, [throwing] his reins on the horse's neck, and [trusting] to the instinct of the animal to find his road" ["The Poet"]). (Perhaps it helps if you think, as he goes on to say, that what carries us through this world is a divine animal. To spell it out, the human is the rational divine animal. It's a thought — one, by the way, which Heidegger would deny.)

This idea of abandonment gives us a way to grasp the act Emerson pictures as "[writing] on the lintels of the door-post, Whim" ("Self-Reliance"). He says he would do this after he has said that he shuns father and mother and wife and brother when his genius calls him; and he follows it by expressing the hope that it is somewhat better than whim at last. (Something has happened; it is up to us to name it, or not to. Something is wrestling us for our blessing.) Whether his writing on the lintels — his writing as such, I gather — is thought of as having the constancy of the contents of a mezuzah or the emergency of the passover blood, either way he is taking upon himself the mark of God, and of departure. His perception of the moment is taken in hope, as something to be proven only on the way, *by* the way. This departure, such setting out, is, in our poverty, what hope consists in, all there is to hope for; it is the abandoning of despair, which is otherwise our condition. (Quiet desperation Thoreau will call it; Emerson had said, silent melancholy.) Hence he may speak of perception as "not Whimsical, but fatal" (ibid.), pre-eminently, here, the perception of what we may call whim. Our fatality, the determination of our fate, of whether we may hope, goes by our marking the path of whim. We hope it is better than whim at last, as we hope we may at last seem something better than blasphemers; but it is our poverty not to be final but always to be leaving (abandoning whatever we have and have known): to be initial, medial, American. What the ground of the fixated conflict between solipsism and realism should give way to—or between subjectivity and objectivity, or the private and the public, or the inner and the outer—is the task of onwardness. In Heidegger: "The *thanc* means man's inmost mind, the heart, the heart's core, that innermost essence of man which reaches outward most fully and to the outermost limits" (*What Is Called Thinking?*). In Emerson: "To believe your own thought, to believe that what is true for you in your private heart, is true for all men—that is genius. Speak your latent conviction and it shall be the universal sense; for always the inmost becomes the outmost" ("Self-Reliance"). The substantive disagreement with Heidegger, shared by Emerson and Thoreau, is that the achievement of the human requires not inhabitation and settlement but abandonment, leaving. Then everything depends upon your realization of abandonment. For the significance of leaving lies in its discovery that you have settled something, that you have felt enthusiastically what there is to abandon yourself to, that you can treat the others there are as those to whom the inhabitation of the world can now be left.

An Emerson Mood

An Emerson Mood

Accepting an honor, a happy public assessment of one's work, grants one a particular opportunity for self-assessment, a moment of perspective from within which to judge not so much the worth of the work as the direction of it, whether it is on the track. In seeking this perspective, in the course of thinking how I might respond in this Scholar's Day address to the honor of the invitation to deliver it, I found myself recurring to the most famous address, and I suppose the best, ever given by an American thinker on a scholar's day, I mean Emerson's "The American Scholar," delivered at Harvard the year Thoreau graduated there, a hundred and forty-two summers ago. Apparently I would like to assess my direction from those high thoughts. Surely this is reasonable, since Emerson and Thoreau may be taken as philosophers of direction, orienters, tirelessly prompting us to be on our way, endlessly asking us where we stand, what it is we face.

Two passages from Emerson especially came to my mind in terms of which, it seemed to me, I might look at all the writing and the teaching I have done until now. The first is from "The American Scholar" (1837):

> I ask not for the great, the remote, the romantic; what is doing in Italy or Arabia; what is Greek art, or Provençal minstrelsy; I embrace the common, I explore and sit at the feet of the familiar, the low. Give me insight into today, and you may have the antique and future worlds. What would we really know the meaning of? The meal in the firkin; the milk in the pan; the ballad in the street; the news of the boat; the glance of the eye; the form and the gait of the body; — show me the ultimate reason of these matters; show me the sublime presence of the highest spiritual cause lurking, as always it does lurk, in these suburbs and extremities of nature; . . . — and the world lies no longer a dull miscellany and lumber-room, but has form and order; there is no trifle, there is no puzzle, but one design unites and animates the farthest pinnacle and the lowest trench.

The second is from the essay that began his reputation, *Nature*, published the year before:

> Give me health and a day, and I will make the pomp of emperors ridiculous. The dawn is my Assyria; the sunset and moonrise my Paphos, and unimaginable realms of faerie; broad noon shall be my England of the senses and the understanding; the night shall be my Germany of mystic philosophy and dreams.

Something Emerson means by the common, the familiar, and the low is something I have meant, from the beginning to the end of the work I have so far accomplished, in my various defenses of proceeding in philosophy from ordinary language, from words of everyday life. In practice this has often meant, especially in the first decade of my writing, defending the procedures, and certain of the views, even, I think, certain of the instincts, in the works of J. L. Austin of Oxford, and in Wittgenstein's *Philosophical Investigations*, which really means attempting to inherit those writings. They remain for me the guiding sources of, at a minimum, what is still known as ordinary language philosophy.

Along with any such inheritance one is likely to inherit intellectual competitors, together with a few guiding obsessions, or investments. I suppose the dominant obsession shared by Austin and Wittgenstein was to provide an answer to skepticism, both with respect to whether we can know that a world of things exists at all, and whether we can know that there are other minds, creatures who share our capacities of consciousness, who are aware of us as we are of them. I had, it is true, already inherited this obsession from the teaching of C. I. Lewis at Harvard and, if I may say so, from Kant (from whom Lewis, and, indirectly, Wittgenstein, had themselves inherited it). But I suppose one inherits in philosophy only what one must recognize as one's own.

Austin's habit of answer was to show, in untiring detail, and in case after case, that philosophers who say things such as that "We do not know with certainty that there are things like tables and chairs because we do not really or literally see them but only see appearances or parts of them" are *not* properly using the words "parts" or "appearances" or "only" or "see" or "literally" or "things" or "know" or "certainty" or "really." If "not properly using" means "not using these words in their ordinary contexts," Austin is perfectly right, and he achieved some dazzling and permanent results in his way of detailing what the ordinary contexts of words are, and systematizing these into several new subjects (e.g., those of speech acts and of excuses). This achievement should make us wonder why this detailing of our lives is something we have to be *made* to do, why it is hard to do.

But as a set of criticisms of philosophy, Austin's results are left quite up in the air; it is not clear that they need matter to a differently inspired philosopher. When Descartes, in his second *Meditation,* takes his famous bit of wax as an example of our knowledge of bodies, one of the results or morals of his investigation is the warning that " . . . words impede me, and I am nearly deceived by the terms of ordinary language. For we say we see the same wax if it is present . . . ," whereas Descartes takes himself to have just now proven that we do not. And Descartes can be as convincing as Austin can be. Wittgenstein, satisfyingly, is at pains to work below this impasse, but his writing is obscure and he has left his critics, as has Austin, with the impression that he writes in support of our ordinary beliefs about the world, our common sense of the world, and hence that he is anti-intellectual, or anyway anti-scientific. What is true is that Wittgenstein is opposed to the effort to make philosophy into science, or into anything else; he insists on the autonomy of philosophy, while at the same time he seeks, as he puts it, to replace philosophy.

As to the prior idea, of Wittgenstein's defending

ordinary beliefs, while this is a significantly wrong idea it is hard to say what is wrong with it. I think it takes Wittgenstein's whole philosophy, at least, to say what is wrong with it, which really comes to presenting the right alternative. Even if an ordinary language philosopher could convince a differently inspired philosopher, or an ordinary human being, that it is not quite right to say that we *believe* the world exists (though certainly we should not conclude that we do *not* believe this, that we *fail* to believe its existence), and wrong even to say we *know* it exists (while of course it is equally wrong to say we fail to know this), he or she would have a hard time saying what it is right to say here, what truly expresses our convictions in the matter. I think this is a genuine and a fruitful perplexity. What the ordinary language philosopher is feeling — but I mean to speak just for myself in this — is that our relation to the world's existence is somehow *closer* than the ideas of believing and knowing are made to convey. If a philosopher says, rather than speaking of our beliefs, that he is examining the meaning or the uses of our words, or investigating our concepts, these descriptions are none too clear themselves, and not clearly more accurate. What still wants expression is a sense that my relation to the existence of the world, or to my existence in the world, is not given in words but in silence. (This would not be a matter of keeping your mouth shut but of understanding when, and how, not to yield to the temptation to say what you do not or cannot exactly mean.)

While I find that this sense of intimacy with existence, or intimacy lost, is fundamental to the experience of what I understand ordinary language philosophy to be, I am for myself convinced that the thinkers who convey this experience best, most directly and most practically, are not such as Austin and Wittgenstein but such as Emerson and Thoreau. This sense of my natural relation to existence is what Thoreau means by our being *next* to the laws of nature, by our *neighboring* the world, by our being *beside* ourselves. Emerson's idea of the *near* is one of the inflections he gives to the common, the low.

An emphasis on the ordinariness of human speech, as opposed to technicalities, whether of science or of logic or of any system of metaphysics, is a recurrent one in philosophy. It is something to see in Socrates at the beginning of philosophy, and in the Northern reformers and the Renaissance Italian Humanists, and in the crises of philosophy throughout the present century. The confrontation of skepticism gives a way of grasping why this emphasis on the ordinary keeps on recurring. Speaking of ordinary or everyday language as *natural* language expresses something we would like to understand as, I might say, a natural relation to nature. It is this relation that the skeptic's doubts distance us from, so that his dissatisfaction in replacing this natural relation with a construction of certainty after the fact is so far a correct dissatisfaction. The recurrent appeal to ordinary or natural language in the history of philosophy is the sign that there is some inner wish of philosophy to escape as well as to recover the natural. I have put this elsewhere by saying that the appeal to ordinary language is an attempt to return the human being to the language of philosophy, as though philosophy is recurrently in danger of banishing it. But I have then gone on to acknowledge that the denial of the human, the

wish to escape the conditions of humanity, call them
conditions of finitude, is itself only human.

By "embracing the common," by "sitting at the feet
of the low," Emerson surely takes his stand on the side
of what philosophers such as Berkeley and Hume would
have called the vulgar. Unlike a certain line of thinkers
from Plato through Nietzsche to Heidegger, for whom
real thinking requires spiritual aristocracy, those English writers will not depart from and disdain the life of
the vulgar. It is internal to their philosophical ambitions to reconcile their philosophical discov-
eries with the views of the vulgar, as Berkeley does
when, for example, he says that his denial of the real
existence of bodies, or corporeal substance, does not
deny the existence and reality of timber, stone, moun-
tains, rivers, when taken *in the vulgar sense* or *in the
vulgar acceptation*, phrases he italicizes. His direct
opponent is rather, as Hume's is, the reputedly sophis-
ticated philosopher. Like Descartes they appeal to
uncorrupted human understanding over the head of
established philosophy.

But Emerson goes rather beyond these reconcilia-
tions and alliances. By "sitting at the feet" of the familiar and the low, this student of Eastern philosophy
must mean that he takes the familiar and the low as his
study, as his guide, his guru; as much his point of
arrival as of departure. In this he joins his thinking with
the new poetry and art of his times, whose topics he
characterizes as "the literature of the poor, the feelings
of the child, the philosophy of the street, the meaning
of household life." He calls this "a great stride," a sign
of new vigor. I note that when he describes himself as

asking "not for the great, the remote, the romantic," he is apparently not considering that the emphasis on the low and the near is exactly the opposite face of the romantic, the continued search for a new intimacy in the self's relation to its world.

In speaking of the near, and praising it as "richer than all foreign parts," this American scholar is also calling upon American scholars to give over their imitations of Europe, to stop turning away from their own inspiration, something which for Emerson is the same matter of our salvation in the intellectual life as it is in the religious life. It is hard to imagine anything more offensive to our pride of intellectual cosmopolitanism than such a call to nativism, or ethnocentrism. One cause of this offense, I should guess, is that it says again that philosophy is not science, which is *the* cosmopolitan, anyway international, means of communication. But a complimentary cause is that it asks us to consider what it is native to us to do, and what is native to philosophy, to thinking. In my own case, my discovery, or rediscovery for myself, of Emerson and of Thoreau seems to me a kind of hearkening to Emerson's call to American scholars. When I ask whether we may not see them as part of our inheritance as philosophers, I am suggesting that our foreignness as philosophers to these writers (and it is hard to imagine any writers more foreign to our currently established philosophical sensibility) may itself be a sign of an impoverished idea of philosophy, of a remoteness from philosophy's origins, from what is native to it, as if a certain constitution of the cosmopolitan might merely consist in a kind of universal provincialism, a worldwide shrinking of the spirit.

In the passage we have taken from "The American Scholar" Emerson says, "Give me insight into today, and you may have the antique and future worlds." In *Nature* he had said, "Give me health and a day, and I will make the pomp of emperors ridiculous." When I first read the ensuing summary of how Emerson proposed (as Thoreau will put it in *Walden*) to "make a day of it," i.e., of his sum of days, how he determined what his dawn and sunset and moonrise will constitute, but especially his saying "broad noon shall be my England of the senses and the understanding; the night shall be my Germany of mystic philosophy and dreams," I felt I had at once a determination of the goal of my private life, the putting together of day and night, of body and soul; and a determination of a task of philosophy, the placing in the same daily cycle of England and of Germany, a task I felt the perspective of America made both possible and necessary. Something like the healing of the rift between the English and the German traditions of philosophy—or failing that, the witnessing of it—has also been a motive of my writing from its earliest to its latest installments. Then a question for me becomes why it took me so long to get my bearings in Emerson.

Before considering that question I remark a feature of Emerson's writing that associates it in my mind with my involvement in the study of film. His list in "The American Scholar" of the matters whose "ultimate reason" he demands of students to know — "'The meal in the firkin; the milk in the pan; the ballad in the street; the news of the boat; the glance of the eye; the form and the gait of the body"—is a list epitomizing what we may call the physiognomy of the ordinary, a form of what Kierkegaard calls the perception of the sublime in the everyday. It is a list, made three or four years before Daguerre will exhibit his copper plates in Paris, epitomizing the obsessions of photography. I once remarked that Baudelaire, in his praise of a painter of modern life, had had a kind of premonition of film. Here I should like to add that without the mode of perception inspired in Emerson (and Thoreau) by the everyday, the near, the low, the familiar, one is bound to be blind to the poetry of film, to the sublimity of it. Naturally I should like to say that this would at the same time insure deafness to some of the best poetry of philosophy — not now its mythological flights, nor its beauty or purity of argumentation, but now its power of exemplification, the world in a piece of wax. If I say that film has become my sunset and moonrise, "my Paphos, and unimaginable realms of faerie," then I must add that Thoreau had become, or returned, my dawn.

Then why did it take me from the time I first remember knowing of Emerson's yoking of day and night and of my sense of implication in his words, until just over a year ago, some two decades later, to begin to look actively at his work, to demand explicitly my inheritance of him?* This is to ask how it happened that I came to feel ready to listen to him. My answer on the present occasion will be to speak less of myself than of Emerson's voice, and first of the voices of philosophy.

Philosophical thinking is not something that a normal human being can submit to all the time, nor at any time he or she may choose. Philosophical questions — say as to whether we can know that God or the world or

* In "Thinking of Emerson," reprinted in this volume.

others exist, or why it is that something exists rather than nothing, or whether we can know that we are not now asleep and dreaming that we are awake, or whether ethical or aesthetic values have an objective basis, or whether mind and body are one thing or two things, or whether men and women are the same or different— are not questions that are alive for one at just any time. And as if in consequence, when they come alive they cannot be put aside as normal questions can be. They drift between the boring and the urgent, or between the remote and the immediate. One image of the unpredictability of the appearance of philosophy is that of Socrates on his way to the symposium, turned aside from normal human intercourse, entranced by the call of his genius to contemplation. Another image of the exclusiveness and the exhaustiveness of the attention philosophy requires is given in the second paragraph of Descartes's *Meditations,* where he speaks of having freed his mind of all kinds of cares: "I feel myself, fortunately, disturbed by no passions; and I have found a serene retreat in peaceful solitude." I should like to speak in this connection of the *mood* of philosophy, a frame of mind in which it is sought, or sought further.

Emerson may be said to be a philosopher of moods and it is one wise with moods who observes that "Our moods do not believe in each other" ("Circles"). Neither do our philosophies, or visions, which is why the ideal of a pluralism in philosophy, however well meant, is so often an empty hope; and neither do our nonphilosophical and our philosophical moods believe in each other. The images I have cited of the philosophical mood in Socrates and in Descartes are images of isolation, of singling oneself, or being singled, out. And we know there is also such a thing as philosophical dialogue. But then isn't *lecturing* about philosophy an extraordinary, even bizarre, activity, neither a time of solitude nor of conversation? If we agree that it is bizarre, then do we know how *writing* philosophy is any the less bizarre? These doubts may usefully raise the question of the audience of philosophy, perhaps in the form of asking how philosophizing is to sound.

The idea of a mood to which philosophical thinking must bring us is still not quite enough to describe my inability for so long to get on with Emerson. His words did not merely strike me as partaking of a mood to which they could not draw me, and hence remained empty to me. They seemed to me repellent, quite as if presenting me with something for which I could not acknowledge my craving. His difference from other philosophical writing is, I think, that it asks the philosophical mood so purely, so incessantly, giving one little other intellectual amusement or eloquence or information, little other argument or narrative, and no other source of companionship or importance, either political or religious or moral, save the importance of philosophy, of thinking itself.

I must take up again a favorite passage of mine from "Self-Reliance," composed a year or two later than "The American Scholar," which I take as a parable of his writing and hence of what he wants of his readers. My first remarks about the passage (in "Thinking of Emerson") have not, I have reason to believe, been successful in conveying the sense that Emerson's writing will, from the outside, seem vague and inflated, but from inside will acquire a terrible exactness. The passage runs as follows:

The doctrine of hatred must be preached, as the counteraction of the doctrine of love, when that pules and whines. I shun father and mother and wife and brother when my genius calls me. I would write on the lintels of the door-post, *Whim*. I hope it is somewhat better than whim at last, but we cannot spend the day in explanation. Expect me not to show cause why I seek or why I exclude company. Then again, do not tell me, as a good man did today, of my obligation to put all poor men in good situations. Are they *my* poor? I tell thee, thou foolish philanthropist, that I grudge the dollar, the dime, the cent I give to such men as do not belong to me and to whom I do not belong.

The general background of substitution could hardly be clearer. What Jesus required of one who would follow him Emerson requires of himself in following his genius — to hate his father, and mother, and wife, and children, and brethren, and sisters, yea, and his own life (Luke 14:26); to recognize that the promise of the kingdom of heaven is not an unconditional promise of peace but a fair warning that the time for decision and division will come. This substitution of self for Jesus, or rather of the self's genius, was not without precedent in this former preacher and the author of the Divinity School Address (1838), with his denunciation of an emphasis on the person of Jesus and on some past, historical revelation. The economy of the passage is also of this background. He would not give money to the poor, who are not *his* poor, for the reason that Jesus will not give words but in parables, because to those who have ears to hear and hear not, and do not understand, it is not given to know the mysteries of the kingdom of heaven; because "for whosoever hath not, from him shall be taken away even that he hath" (Matthew 13:12–13). Hard sayings; but no harder than the fact that he is the one he is and that each of us is the one each of us is.

But it is the foreground of the passage that I wish to focus on, its setting of a certain scene of writing. I understand the writer to be accounting both for the fact of his writing and for what he writes. When his genius calls him and he divides himself from society he does not write on the lintels of the door-post "my genius calls me." Or does he? Does he write "Whim"? He says he *would*. Why would he? Because, I gather, that is all this scrupulous epistemologist of moods would claim to know. The call of one's genius presents itself with no deeper authority than whim. And what presents itself in the form of whim is bound sometimes to be exactly whim and nothing more. (Or worse. In the paragraph preceding this one Emerson had remembered, when young, being cautioned by a valued advisor that his inner impulses may be from below, not from above, and remembered being prompted to reply: "They do not seem to me to be such; but if I am the Devil's child, I will live then from the Devil.") He hopes it is somewhat better than whim at last—for as with prophecy you can only know the true from the false by its fruits. When later in the essay he says that "perception is not whimsical, but fatal" (where perception is the organ to which whim occurs) he is saying that something which is of the least importance, which has no importance whatever but for the fact that it is mine, that it has occurred to me, becomes by that fact alone of the last importance; it constitutes my fate; it is a matter of my life and death. If we could know in advance of departure after whim that it will truly prove to have been our genius that has called us, then the gate to salvation would not be strait; there would be little need for faith, and little to write about. But why does he mark whim on the lintels of his door-post? Why mark anything?

We may understand this marking to invoke the passover blood, and accordingly again see writing as creating a division — between people we may call Egyptians and those we may call Jews — which is a matter of life and death, of the life and death of one's first-born.

But literal writing on the door-posts of one's house is more directly a description of the mezuzah (a small piece of parchment inscribed with two passages from Deuteronomy and marked with a name of God, which may be carried as an amulet but which is more commonly seen slanted on the door frame of a dwelling as a sign that a Jewish family lives within). (The spiritual danger in putting Whim in place of the name of God will seem a small thing to one convinced that the name of God is mostly taken in the place of whim.) According ingly we should consider that the writing contained in the mezuzah explains why the mezuzah is there, why God has commanded that it be there. We are told in each of the passages it contains to obey God's commandments, particularly in view of the land we are to possess, of milk and honey. "Therefore shall ye lay up these my words in your heart and in your soul, and bind them for a sign upon your hand, that they may be as frontlets between your eyes. And ye shall teach them to your children, speaking of them when thou sittest in thine house, and when thou walkest by the way, and when thou liest down, and when thou risest up. And thou shalt write them upon the door posts of thine house. . . ." So it is in obedience to Emerson's genius that he speaks of it wherever he is, showing that it speaks everywhere to him; not to acknowledge it would be not to keep faith with it. As if his essays were so many mezuzahs, declarations of his faith, and his part in attempting to keep this land of milk and honey from perishing.

(Here I must pause for the pleasure of identifying the title of one of the recent films I care most about as occurring in the mezuzah, *Days of Heaven.* "As the days of heaven upon the earth" is the phrase used in the King James version to describe our stay "in the land which the Lord sware unto your fathers to give them" — *if*, that is to say, we keep faith with the word of the covenant. Several reviewers of this film have felt that it has something to do with the story of America. The source of its title specifies the phase of the story as one in which this promised land, in forgetting its faith and serving foreign gods, lies under a threat. It has been sent the plague of locusts; it has been warned; and this film, in the prophetic tradition of American literature, takes up the warning. As the land was given, on condition, so it can be taken away.)

To speak of Emerson's essays as the contents of new mezuzahs is to imply that he has written on the lintels of his door-posts both Whim and the knowledge that his genius has called him, for the essays are the fruits by which his prophetic whim is to be known. Thus have I given something of the explanation he claimed we cannot spend the day in. Considering what he means by a day in our opening two texts, that it is the measure of our lives, he is saying that to begin to explain would be to spend his life in explanation. But then this is my occasion, not his, which was to verify what I named his epistemology of the call of his genius. There are always good reasons not to obey this call, not to verify it. From its beginning, from its presenting itself as whim, it follows that there must be obligations which it prompts you to leap over; there is always something to do first, something to say first before preaching the kingdom of heaven; for example, there are those at your house to whom to bid farewell, or there may be dead to bury (Luke 9:59–62). And as for the poor, it took a brave man then, and a braver one now, if he is righteous, to imply that he has the poor with him always, but the call of his genius he has not always (Mark 4:7).

Will this priority of a certain whim (to departure) over a certain obligation (to remain) not make a person rootless, and nowadays for nothing more than selfish reasons, which you may call religious but which religion is not likely to teach? And isn't there something especially troubling here in an American? True, this was to be the land where the individual could grow freely, wildly if he or she wished; but it was also a place to which strangers could come to put down roots, the place to which pilgrims and immigrants come home. Whereas when Emerson seems to say that he is responsible only for what he calls *his* poor, for such as belong to him and to whom he belongs, he suggests that responsibility is his to pick up or to put down. As if sinking roots is not a matter of finding out where you want to live but finding out what wants to live in you.*
As if your roots—that is, your origins—are matters

---

* Along with the association to Terrence Malick's *Days of Heaven*, I should like to make explicit associations to three other friends as I was composing these pages—to a conversation with Robert Nozick on the idea of roots, and to an understanding with John Hollander about

not of the past but precisely of the present, always, fatally. As if America could banish history, could make of the condition of immigrancy not something to escape from but something to aspire to, as to the native human condition.

I am not unaware that this may sound like one of those Transcendentalist sublimities which I confessed a while ago has seemed repellent to me, no doubt significantly because they may seem so easy for someone to voice who has Emerson's connections. But whatever needs rebuke and explanation here, this is not my present mood, or I will not, if I can help it, call upon this mood. I am at present surprised to find two other questions coming to mind: first whether that remark about immigrancy as the native human condition is something my immigrant father, dead three years this January, could have ever understood; and second whether the note of finding what is native to you, where this turns out to mean shunning the cosmopolitan and embracing the immigrant in yourself, is one a professor should strike. These are matters about which one cannot claim expertise, nothing for which a degree is a credential. Evidently the joining of these questions of what my father would be in a position to understand and of what I find myself in a position to say to students is meant to join a question as to the authority of one's address.

But the authority of making one's mark is just the

Emerson's passage that puts together England and Germany, and to exchanges with Burton Dreben on the position in which the work of analytical philosophy, and especially the work of such as Austin and Wittgenstein, has placed the reasonable expectations of the subject of philosophy.

question Emerson, for all his connections, is raising in his parable of writing Whim on his door-posts. It is written in a certain hope and in posing the issue of what he is to own, dividing those who belong to him and to whom he belongs from all others, asking who his poor are and hence who his rich are, and so who his honorable and dishonorable are, and who his beautiful and his ugly, his inspirers and his dispiriters. . . . It is agreeing to make a day not of explanation but of judgment. How can this be easier or harder for him than for any man or woman? It is frightening to be called upon to do, to further "the conversion of the world" ("The American Scholar"). And yet Emerson clearly regards himself as exercising the duties of the American scholar, i.e., of Man Thinking, which he finds to be comprised in self-trust, soon to be renamed by him self-reliance. Along with guiding men, the office of the scholar is to cheer and to raise them. How can you cheer and raise them by frightening them?

Let us recall that Emerson depicts his immediate and constant audience as the young scholar or student (which, as he and Thoreau never tire of saying, is a capacity residing in each human being, the best part, even the essential, of the human being), and in particular depicts them, in "The American Scholar," as disgusted by the principles on which the world is managed, or ready to die of disgust, and in "Self-Reliance" as losing heart. Presumably our students have lost heart in failing, in another phrase of "Self-Reliance," to obey their heart; and presumably they would not have failed in this obedience unless it were frightening. Not difficult to do, but difficult to let yourself do. Once you do it it is easy; but everything conspires against it. It is a matter of taking back to yourself an authority for yourself you have been compelled to invest elsewhere. So the matter of authority is as much one of hearing as it is one of uttering—as Emerson's parable shows to have been his case as well. It is not up to him to create your whim for you, nor to create your mood of philosophy. His experience tells him—the thing that expertise can never know—that the whim and the mood are bound to occur. (Thoreau will call such things "opportunities," and say of them that there never is more than one of a kind.) His record is there, his prose in conversation with itself, dutifully watching for our participation, or our refusal of it. It does not require us. That is itself its guidance. We are at liberty to discover whether he belongs to us and we to him. We, who have already failed to obey the heart; and he, who has already succeeded, are to meet at a common origin. To say, "Follow me and you will be saved," you must be sure you are of God. But to say, "Follow in yourself what I follow in mine and you will be saved," you merely have to be sure you are following yourself. This frightens and cheers me.

Design by David Bullen
Typeset in Mergenthaler Plantin
by Accent & Alphabet
Printed by Braun-Brumfield
on acid-free paper